HOW TO START MIND MAPPING

YOUR COMPREHENSIVE GUIDE TO BOOST YOUR
MEMORY, BUILD RAZOR-SHARP FOCUS,
SUPERCHARGE YOUR PRODUCTIVITY AND
UNLOCK YOUR CREATIVE POTENTIAL

WISDOM UNIVERSITY

CONTENTS

Get ALL our upcoming eBooks for FREE
(Yes, you've read that right)
Total Value: $199.80*

You'll get exclusive access to our books before they hit the online shelves and enjoy them for free.

Additionally, you'll receive the following bonuses:

Bonus Nr. 1

Our Bestseller
How To Train Your Thinking
Total Value: $9.99

If you're ready to take maximum control of your finances and career, then keep reading...

Here's just a fraction of what you'll discover inside:
- Why hard work has almost nothing to do with making money, and what the real secret to wealth is
- Why feeling like a failure is a great place to start your success story
- The way to gain world-beating levels of focus, even if you normally struggle to concentrate

"This book provides a wealth of information on how to improve your thinking and your life. It is difficult to summarize the information provided. When I tried, I found I was just listing the information provided on the contents page. To obtain the value provided in the book, you must not only read and understand the provided information, you must apply it to your life."

NealWC - Reviewed in the United States on July 16, 2023

"This is an inspirational read, a bit too brainy for me as I enjoy more fluid & inspirational reads. However, the author lays out the power of thought in a systematic way!"

Esther Dan - Reviewed in the United States on July 13, 2023

"This book offers clear and concise methods on how to think. I like that it provides helpful methods and examples about the task of thinking. An insightful read for sharpening your mind."

Demetrius - Reviewed in the United States on July 16, 2023

"Exactly as the title says, actionable steps to guide your thinking! Clear and concise."

Deirdre Hagar Virgillo - Reviewed in the United States on July 18, 2023

"This is a book that you will reference for many years to come. Very helpful and a brain changer in you everyday life, both personally and professionally. Enjoy!"

Skelly - Reviewed in the United States on July 6, 2023

Bonus Nr. 2

Our Bestseller
The Art Of Game Theory
Total Value: $9.99

If Life is a game, what are the rules? And more importantly... Where are they written?

Here's just a fraction of what you'll discover inside:

- When does it pay to be a selfish player... and why you may need to go inside a prisoner's mind to find out
- How to recognize which game you're playing and turn the tables on your opponent... even if they appear to have the upper hand
- Why some games aren't worth playing and what you should do instead

"Thanks Wisdom University! This book offers simple strategies one can use to achieve things in your personal life. Anyone of average intelligence can read, understand and be in a position to enact the suggestions contained within."

David L. Jones - Reviewed in the United States on November 12, 2023

"Haven't finished it yet, but what I've gone through so far is just incredible! Another great job from this publisher!"

W. S. Jones - Reviewed in the United States on October 12, 2023

"A great book to help you through difficult and complex problems. It gets you to think differently about what you are dealing with. Highly recommend to both new and experienced problem solvers. You with think differently after reading this book."

Thom - Reviewed in the United States on October 18, 2023

"I like this book and how it simplifies complex ideas into something to use in everyday life. I am applying the concept and gaining a lot of clarity and insight."

Ola - Reviewed in the United States on October 18, 2023

"The book is an excellent introduction to game theory. The writing is clear, and the analysis is first-rate. Concrete, real-world examples of theory are presented, and both the ways in which game theory effectively models what actually happens in life is cogently evaluated. I also appreciate the attention paid to the ethical dimensions of applying game theory in many situations."

Amazon Customer - Reviewed in the United States on October 8, 2023

Bonus Nr. 3 & 4

Thinking Sheets
Break Your Thinking Patterns
&
Flex Your Wisdom Muscle
Total Value Each: $4.99

A glimpse into what you'll discover inside:

- How to expose the sneaky flaws in your thinking and what it takes to fix them (the included solutions are dead-simple)
- Dozens of foolproof strategies to make sound and regret-free decisions leading you to a life of certainty and fulfillment
- How to elevate your rationality to extraordinary levels (this will put you on a level with Bill Gates, Elon Musk and Warren Buffett)
- Hidden gems of wisdom to guide your thoughts and actions (gathered from the smartest minds of all time)

Here's everything you get:

✓ How To Train Your Thinking eBook   ($9.99 Value)
✓ The Art Of Game Theory eBook   ($9.99 Value)
✓ Break Your Thinking Patterns Sheet   ($4.99 Value)
✓ Flex Your Wisdom Muscle Sheet   ($4.99 Value)
✓ All our upcoming eBooks   ($199.80* Value)

Total Value: $229.76

Go to wisdom-university.net for the offer!

(Or simply scan the code with your camera)

Scan Me

*If you download 20 of our books for free, this would equal a value of 199.80$

WHAT READER'S ARE SAYING ABOUT
WISDOM UNIVERSITY

"I have been reading books from Wisdom University for a while now and have been impressed with the CONDENSED AND VALUABLE INFORMATION they contain. Reading these books allows me to LEARN INFORMATION QUICKLY AND EASILY, so I can put the knowledge to practice right away to improve myself and my life. I recommend it for busy people who don't have a LOT of time to read, but want to learn: Wisdom University gives you the opportunity to easily and quickly learn a lot of useful, practical information, which helps you have a better, more productive, successful, and happier life. It takes the information and wisdom of many books and distills and organizes the most useful and helpful information down into a smaller book, so you spend more time applying helpful information, rather than reading volumes of repetition and un-needed filler text.

—Dawn Campo, Degree in Human psychology and Business, Office administrator from Utah

"WU is a provider of books regarding mental models, thought processes, organizational systems, and other forms of mental optimization. The paradigmatic customer likely is to be someone in an early- to mid-career stage, looking to move up the ranks. Ultimately, though, the books could be of use to everyone from high school students to accomplished executives looking for ways to optimize and save time."

—Matthew Staples, 45, Texas (USA), Juris Doctor, Attorney

"I have most of the ebooks & audiobooks that Wisdom University has created. I prefer audiobooks as found on Audible. The people comprising Wisdom University do an excellent job of providing quality personal development materials. They offer value for everyone interested in self-improvement."

—*Neal Cheney, double major in Computer-Science & Mathematics, retired 25yrs USN (Nuclear Submarines) and retired Computer Programmer*

"I would recommend these books to my grandson."

—Daniel, Florida (USA), 69, Bachelor Degree, retired

"Wisdom University embodies an innovative and progressive educational approach, expertly merging deep academic insights with contemporary learning techniques. Their books are not only insightful and captivating but also stand out for their emphasis on practical application, making them a valuable resource for both academic learning and real-world personal development."

—Bryan Kornele, 55 years old, Software Engineer from the United States

"WU's emails discuss interesting topics. They have good offers. I can recommend the books to my My friends and relatives."

—Wilbur Dudley, Louisiana (USA), 77, BS in Business Administration and DBA, retired

"I wanted to read some books about thinking and learning which have some depth. I can say "Wisdom University" is one of the most valuable and genuine brands I have ever seen. Their books are top-notch at kindle. I have read their books on learning, thinking, etc. & they are excellent. I would especially recommend their latest book "Think Like Da Vinci" to those who want to have brilliant & clear thinking."

—Sahil Zen, 20 years old from India, BSc student of Physics

"Wisdom University's works provide a synthesis of different books giving a very good summary and resource of self-help topics. I have recommended them to someone who wanted to learn about a topic and in the least amount of time."

—Travvis Mahrer, BA in Philosphy, English Teacher in a foreign country

INTRODUCTION

The picture above tells a story. Did you get it?

Of course, you did. One look at the picture [1] above, and we all have the same literary selection in mind. A nursery rhyme with a fiddling cat, a laughing dog, a dish and a spoon running away together, and a cow – well, you know.

There is a reason why children love picture books. Their colorful, animated images set the stage for the words on the page to come alive with meaning. Children learn most from what they see, and this is not surprising. Vision is generally considered our most important and most complex sense, as much socially and culturally as it is biologically. [2] A great portion of all individuals who have the benefit of sight are predominantly visual learners, which accounts for our minds' strong affinity to visual information. [3]

Not only children are attracted to pictures, but adults as well, both young and old. Who has not preferred an illustrated version of a novel in high school, or an atlas or magazine with glossy photographs while traveling or passing the time away? When my students were tasked to read *Les Miserables*, the renowned novel by Victor Hugo, almost all of them opted to watch the award-winning movie starring the popular actors, Hugh Jackman and Russell Crowe.

Much of what we learn is, therefore, stored in our minds in the form of images. Frequently, we communicate what we think through words, whether spoken or written. Those who hear or read our words form their own mental images of them. Often, the images they visualize are reasonable reproductions of those in our minds, which completes the communication process. But at times, due to the sender's poor choice of words or inadequate comprehension on the part of the receiver, the images in the minds of the sender and receiver do not match, and miscommunication takes place.

Aside from clarifying our thoughts to others, there is sometimes the need to clarify our thoughts for ourselves. Occasionally, we would think to ourselves, "I need to clear the cobwebs in my head," after which we would go bowling, watch a movie, or indulge in some form of distraction. This is because our minds work in ways science has not yet fully fathomed. Often, difficult problems would leave us hopelessly discombobulated – only for us to cry out, "Eureka!" when, like a bolt of lightning, we are surprised by the right answer lurking all the while in the recesses of our brain. And all the while, we never knew that we knew the answer all along.

There is a systematic way we could probe our brain's contents to flush out the knowledge we did not know we knew. First, define the central topic we wish to flesh out. Second, enumerate the bits of information related to this central topic that we already know, or would want to know more about. Third, develop these bits of information further with supporting data gathered from research and link them up with each other and the main topic. Finally, write all of these down to create a permanent record.

There are many ways to do this, such as by creating an outline or tabulating the information. A range of note-taking methods can be used to gather and organize information. However, the resulting mass of words can be wieldy and just as confusing as the problem it aims to solve. So what if, like a nursery rhyme, a picture can be drawn that conveys the complete information at one glance? That would cut through all the confusion and streamline the message with clarity and precision.

In this book, we will learn about such a method, known as mind mapping. The term is as straightforward as the method it stands for – a map of the mind or, more precisely, a map of our mind's thoughts about a single topic. We should remember that our minds are so complex that there is no way we can fully map them out, either physiologically or virtually. But delimiting the map to a single main topic is as practicable as it is useful – seeing with our eyes an image that represents a thought that is intangible and invisible.

The first chapters of the book introduce the mind mapping method and how it mimics the workings of the brain. Memory-enhancement techniques are presented to aid in effective mind mapping. An examination of some benefits and drawbacks of mind maps is dovetailed by illustrating how to create them. Thereafter, the different uses and forms of mind maps are discussed.

In the penultimate chapter, the detailed construction of a full-blown mind map with its sub-maps is carried out and rendered in two forms: as a spider map, and as a flow diagram. The topic of the illustrative mind map is a section of Chapter 2, the discussion of brain functionalities, so we could follow the process step-by-step. Finally, seven of the more popular digital mind mapping applications are introduced together with their features.

Mind mapping provides so many opportunities for diverse groups of users – students, teachers, professionals, employees, hobbyists, planners, entrepreneurs, and workers. This book only scratches the surface of what mind mapping holds in store for those who are adventurous enough to explore its many potentials. It is therefore ideal for those encountering mind mapping for the first time.

For readers who are already informed on mind mapping and habitually practice it, the chapters that follow are intended to deepen our appreciation of the technique's alignment with human psychology. The final chapter also provides updates on the more recent mind mapping apps.

To be sure, mind mapping is a method that poses challenges for those who wish to master its technicalities. However, the rewards of doing so could greatly benefit all who can successfully tame the immense powers of this mental tool.

Are you ready to unlock mind mapping's world of possibilities? Then turn the page and let us begin.

Dianna Gene P. Aquino

For Jan and Bernadette Schroller

1

THE BIRTH OF MIND MAPS

TRACING THE NON-LINEAR EVOLUTION OF VISUAL THOUGHT AND HOW IT'S SIMILAR TO HOW OUR MIND WORKS

Peanuts' Lucy Van Pelt [1]

"Snap out of it! Five cents, please."

Lucy van Pelt is the sassy character in Charles Schultz's *Peanuts* syndicated comic strip that ran for half a century. The beloved characters not only elicited laughter from readers, but more importantly, they mirrored what we see and experience about ourselves. A running gag was Lucy's psychiatry booth. Its hilarity is derived from the fact that, while children typically run lemonade stands for pocket money, Lucy operated a sidewalk psychiatry clinic. She would dispense simple, pragmatic advice for a professional fee of five cents. Remarkably, the other Peanuts characters consulted with her despite her lack of proper credentials.

Lucy's advice was humorous because it was always useless. When Charlie Brown consulted her about his feelings of depression, she retorted: "Go home and eat a jelly bread sandwich folded over." Once, Lucy consulted herself, sitting alternately at both sides of her booth. Her "doctor self" once counseled her "patient self," "You're cracking up!" [2]

Why We Don't Know How Our Mind Thinks

We might find that last comic situation hysterical – imagine Lucy, the psychiatrist, not knowing what is in her mind – except that it hews closely to reality! Even when we are in the best of mental health, we seldom, if ever, know what goes on in our minds.[3] The reason for this is that the brain works in a roundabout manner that can be approximated by a series of steps.

First, information about outside stimuli enters our sensory system. Our brain then builds a model or simulation, a "simplified, 'quick-and-dirty' version" [4] because our brain has access to this information, we can talk or communicate our observation. Beyond that, however, our conscious experience resonates with an internal, intuitive model that we have constructed at a level deeper than our higher cognition – our subconscious model. Both the conscious and subconscious models are simplifications of the truth that we experience from the outside world. In both cases, they are not the truth but are constructs of our brain created from the information it received.

"Literally, physically, the brain processes information through the interaction of billions of neurons. But when we introspect, when we dip into our intuitions and thinking, we report something totally different – not electrical impulses and synapses, not interacting chunks of information, but something amorphous and ghost-like." – Michael Graziano, professor of psychology and neuroscience at Princeton University [5]

There are instances when the disparity between reality and our perception of it, as described by Graziano, causes us to behave in ways that appear illogical. Take the case of Cindy, who is terrified of entering a McDonald's store. One sight of the cheerful Ronald, with red curly hair, a wide grin, and large funny shoes, causes her to freeze in her tracks and avert her eyes. With cold, sweaty palms, ashen-faced, Cindy would whisper in a small voice that she'd just wait for us outside. She would rather sit by herself for half an hour in the sweltering heat rather than come into the air-conditioned store. Leaving her outside was not an act of child abuse. Cindy is 32 years old.

When she was five, Cindy was watching a series of Disney animated short films recorded on a VHS tape. In between films, a snippet of Stephen King's "*IT*" unexpectedly played. It showed Pennywise, the evil clown around whom the horror movie revolved. The short clip was enough to sear into the mind of an impressionable toddler with a lasting horrific image of the clown to represent all clowns.

Pennywise [6] Versus Ronald McDonald [7]

From then on, while others her age would see a cheerful Ronald McDonald mascot and gleefully enjoy the store's fare, toys, giveaways, and play area, the same clown image would evoke feelings of repulsion in Cindy's mind.

Most people will be exposed to the same stimulus (reality) and build roughly the same mental model (a clown with red hair, a white face, red and yellow attire, and large red shoes). A few will associate the same visual representation with an entirely different intuitive model that they have built deep in their brains. What is a funny character for us is a monster for Cindy.

We all think that because of our inner senses, we have access to our thoughts and therefore know ourselves better. But some disagree. According to Gilbert Ryle, a mid-20th century behaviorist philosopher, we learn about how our minds think by observing our behavior, and that our friends might know our minds better than we do.[8]

Take, for instance, those moments when you were in your teens and, while you were in the company of friends, you chanced to meet a person on whom you had a secret crush. Friends would notice sudden shifts in your behavior, such as speechlessness, shifting your gaze downward, or stealing glances at the object of your affection, and blushing at the cheeks. These behavioral cues may have escaped you but not your friends. Your friends may have known what you were thinking even before you did, and which you may vehemently deny after they would tease you about it.

Storytelling To Motivate

Another clue about how we think we may be oblivious to is how we could be motivated to think a certain way without external pressure, coercion, or intentional persuasion. Paul Zak discovered two decades ago that trust can be signaled by the production of a neurochemical called oxytocin in the brain.[9] Oxytocin is produced when we are shown kindness or when we are trusted, resulting in a desire to cooperate with others. The substance enhances our ability to experience others' emotions, or empathy. Social creatures need empathy because it enables them to understand how others react to a situation, thus creating bonds among individuals.

Knowing this, Zak and his team explored how the oxytocin in the brain may be stimulated to motivate people to engage in cooperative behavior. They experimented, in particular, with the effect of storytelling by playing short video narratives before a target group of respondents, rather than resorting to face-to-face interactions. The researchers drew blood from the respondents before and after the video shows and tested them for oxytocin levels. The result? "Character-driven stories do consistently cause oxytocin synthesis. Further, the amount of oxytocin released by the brain predicted how much people were willing to help others" [10] such as donating money to the charity mentioned in the videos encouraging them to support such charities.

Moreover, to motivate its audience, a story must sustain attention by developing tension during the storytelling. When the right tension is created, the attentive audience empathizes with the characters in it. Even after the story ends, they are likely to mimic the feelings and behavior of the characters in the story. This process constitutes the neurobiology of storytelling. The brain responds to stimuli generated by its sensory areas. Chemical substances are released, and circuits are triggered in the various parts of the brain that produce certain emotions, memories, and actions. In an organizational work setting, the management may have intentionally created the stimuli that elicit these desired reactions. [11] The science behind the thinking process is described in greater detail in the next chapter.

For now, we recognize that our brains make implicit associations among stimuli and construct knowledge based on these associations. Linkages that our brains make are very similar to the connections in the mind maps that help us learn, understand, and retain information about the world around us.

How Mind Mapping Mimics Our Thinking

What do the brain's functions have to do with mind mapping? First, we should get acquainted with mind mapping as a process. Mind mapping is a visual tool we use to capture and organize our thoughts. A picture is worth a thousand words, so let us see what a mind map looks like.

Tennis Mind Map [12]

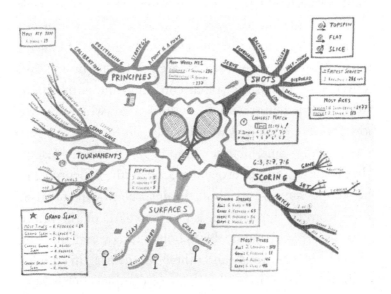

Tennis enthusiasts who take one look at the diagram above know exactly what it is about, and acquire much information from it that they would consider relevant. Mind maps have a central theme, and tennis is the theme of the one above. Surrounding the central theme are bits and pieces of information hierarchically connected to sub-themes. The connections branch out into greater detail, and the result is a visual diagram of the related concepts organized in a manner that allows us to make sense of the central theme.

Mind maps offer a comprehensive overview and delve into extensive information, mirroring the brain's intuitive and creative use of natural associations. [13]

Mind maps mimic the electrochemical activity between brain cells. One of the most common types of brain cells is called neurons. Neurons are nerve cells that transmit messages using electrical and chemical signals. They send information between various areas of the brain, and between the brain, the spinal cord, and the entire body. Most neuroscientists used to think that when we are born, we are equipped with all the neurons we will ever have during our lifetimes. In 1962, however, Joseph Altman discovered neurogenesis, the birth of neurons, in the hippocampus of adult brains. Newborn neurons travel from the hippocampus to other parts of the brain. In the 1980s, Fernando Nottebohm discovered that the number of neurons and their pathways in adults' forebrains – the areas that control complex behavior – can increase dramatically when learning becomes crucial. [14]

Let's see what a neuron looks like.

Complete Neuron Cell Diagram [15]

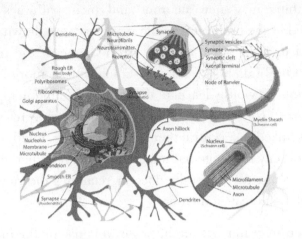

This diagram illustrates the parts of a neuron. We will examine these parts in the next chapter, but for now suffice it to know that neuroscientists observed more neurons are created when learning is intensified. However, the neurons themselves do not store information. Information is stored in the circuits connecting these neurons. It is the networks formed by specific connections between the neurons that help us remember things. [16] More learning increases the neurons, the pathways between them, and the chemical and electrical reactions.

So, how are mind mapping and the brain's workings similar? For one, the resemblance in the structures of neurons, the building blocks of the brain, and mind maps are immediately evident. The web-like connections among the themes in a mind map appear identical to the brain's neural circuits. The incremental manner by which they are developed is likewise similar. When we learn something new, new neurons and their pathways are created in the brain, just as the new topics are drawn and linked to each other and the main theme in the mind map. Our brain associates new stimuli with memories and concepts previously learned, the same way mind mapping organizes concepts by associating them with relevant topics linked to a central theme. Furthermore, mind maps use not only language but imagery, color, and other visual devices, just as the brain does in retaining the sensory stimuli that create a memory.

A mind map mirrors the intricate workings of the brain, organizing information in a radial, non-linear fashion. It visually represents your thoughts, employing associations, connections, and triggers to ignite a cascade of new ideas. [17]

The History Of Mind Mapping

Even if we may have never used a mind map before, we can readily appreciate the usefulness of a visual diagram that organizes ideas and presents them comprehensively in a compact manner. Research suggests that 65 percent of the general population are visual learners – they need to see the information to commit it to memory. [18] Moreover, the brain can process images and videos 60,000 times faster than text, and 90 percent of the information transmitted to the brain is visual. [19] This makes mind mapping a powerful tool for learning and memorizing.

Mind mapping, as a technique, did not happen overnight. It developed for almost two millennia from its austere beginnings centuries ago. While Tony Buzan, the popular psychologist, is the acknowledged creator of modern mind mapping, the godfather of the concept behind the technique was arguably a third-century Greek philosopher and logician known as Porphyry of Tyros. Born in 234 CE, Porphyry sought to classify Aristotle's *Categories* and, in the process, invented the Arbor Porphyriana or Tree of Porphyry [20] (aka the Porphyrian tree), shown in the diagram below. *Categories* was one of Aristotle's greatest works, and Porphyry was tasked to write an introduction to it. To get a comprehensive understanding and better formulate his own ideas of Aristotle's concepts, Porphyry devised a method of visual representation that logically relates these abstractions.

Porphyry's Tree [21]

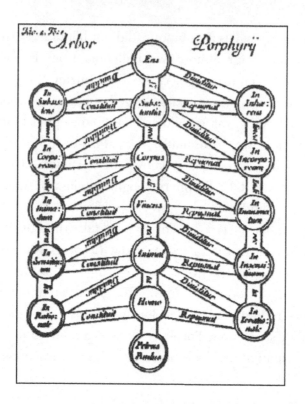

A bit about Aristotle's Categories: it is a part of Aristotle's Organon, the collection of Aristotle's six works on logical analysis and dialectic. Categories is not by itself very long, but it does consist of fifteen chapters, and is "perhaps the single most heavily discussed of all Aristotelian notions." [22] In this treatise, Aristotle sought to place every object of human understanding under one of ten categories, enumerating anything that can be either the subject or the predicate of a proposition. That is practically everything existing or conceived of that can be named. There are ten categories, which we briefly enumerate as substance, quantity, qualification, relative, where, when being-in-a-position, having, doing, and being-affected. [23]

We will go no further, lest we get caught up in the maze of heavy philosophical discussions that have accumulated around this topic since before the third century BCE. But you can see the breadth and complexity of Aristotle's concepts in this one treatise. Porphyry certainly struggled to fully comprehend the important concepts in the Categories. His efforts yielded more than the compressed version of the treatise, but also the rudiments of what we now know as mind mapping.

Action Steps

According to psychology professor Paul Zak, storytelling is a powerful way to motivate how we think without the need to pressure, coerce, or persuade. There are different kinds of stories to motivate different audiences. The following are the short versions of popular stories. Do you think these stories would effectively influence how people think? Which audience would they most strongly influence, and how do you think they would react?

1. Michael Jordan missed more than 9,000 shots in his career and lost almost 300 games. He missed the game-winning shot on 26 occasions. Today he attributes his success to his many repeated failures. [24]

2. The shepherd boy saw a real wolf prowling about his flock. Alarmed, he yelled, "Wolf! Wolf!" at the top of his lungs. But the villagers thought he was trying to fool them

again, and so they stayed in their houses and did not run to his aid.

3. Bernard Madoff was revered as a successful hedge-fund manager and respected NASDAQ chairman. He later confessed to swindling his investors and lost an estimated $65 billion of their money. Madoff was sentenced to 150 years in prison. His older son committed suicide and his younger son died of cancer. Divorced and alone, Madoff died in prison at 86 years.

4. On the fifth day after they lost all their supplies, the group of campers lost in the woods woke up to discover their hiking boots dry and clean of mud, a few cans of stew, and dry firewood outside their tents. Intrigued, Thomas set out in the direction he had seen the glowing figure run the night before. Soon he came to a deep ravine where he saw a tattered backpack, an ancient pair of shoes, and the remains of a camper lost decades ago.
25

Moving On

Throughout our lives, our minds determine what we think, do, and feel. All of the noble and despicable deeds and works in history were born of the minds of humans, yet we do not fully grasp how we think and why we think that way. Mind maps enable us to comprehend the bits and pieces of information we receive in a holistic sense. The following chapter will give us a glimpse into the scientific workings of the brain and how it enables us to think.

Key Takeaways

1. We seldom know how our mind thinks because our brain works in a roundabout manner. What we subconsciously think of is reflected in our behavior, which is more apparent to outside observers than ourselves.
2. Through storytelling and other similar methods, we may be motivated to think in certain ways without external pressure, coercion, or intentional persuasion.
3. Mind mapping mimics the way we think using natural associations. Pieces of information are related to one another, and new learnings are integrated with previous knowledge stored in long-term memory.
4. Famed psychologist Tony Buzan is the father of modern mind mapping, but the technique was first applied in 234 CE by the ancient Greek philosopher, Porphyry of Tyros.

2
___

THE SCIENCE OF MIND MAPPING

UNDERSTANDING THE THEORY OF MIND, LINGUISTIC CONVENTIONS, AND MULTIFACETED BRAIN DYNAMICS

"The most courageous act is still to think for yourself. Aloud." – Coco Chanel [1]

"Penny for your thoughts" is an expression we would use to coax a pensive friend or companion into sharing his or her musings. Sometimes, even without words, we could instinctively guess the deepest thoughts of friends with whom we are unusually close. Spouses who have lived lifetimes together intuitively sense each other's sentiments. BFFs spontaneously respond to each other's telltale signs of joy or despondency.

On the other hand, there are people who we can only describe as "dense" or clueless. Ladies may frequently drop hints that they fancy a particular gentleman, but detect no positive response from the object of their affection. The presence, or absence, of this penchant for discerning what goes on in others' hidden thoughts, is the domain of the theory of mind.

The Theory Of Mind

"Theory of Mind" (TOM) is a concept in cognitive science (or the study of how we think) that refers to our ability to accurately understand how other people are thinking and feeling – their mental states. Mental states fall into numerous diverse classes, including thoughts, beliefs, desires, memories, intentions, perceptions, emotions, and the experiences related to them.

Simply stated, theory of mind refers to how we can correctly connect with other people's thinking. It can be likened to the rational counterpart of emotional empathy. The skills necessary to understand both our own and other people's mental states enable us to predict or explain people's behavior. We gain a heightened potential for social interaction and reciprocal exchange when we develop these "mind-reading" or "mentalizing" skills.

The good news is that almost all of us possess and exhibit them beyond early childhood. But very young children are still unable to understand mental states because they are by nature egocentric and are still unaware of how others might think or feel. [2]

After my first child turned two years old, I returned to my corporate job, leaving him during the day with my mother. I would call home during the lunch break just to check in on them and see how things were going. During one of those calls, my mom handed over the phone to Arnold who excitedly crowed, "Mom! Look at what Granny gave me!" It was followed by five seconds of silence. "See?" he suddenly said. See what? I thought to myself. "What is it, son?" I said aloud. "This! I'm showing it to you!" "Oh, that's nice, baby! Could you hand me back to Granny?"

When my mom came back on the line, I asked what he was talking about. "I gave him a Mickey Mouse stuffed toy. He was 'showing' it to you over the phone." Except that, unlike our present mobile phones, the phones then had no screens. My two-year-old son had no concept of my point of view, and how I might see things from my end. He only knows how things look like from his end.

So how do children develop the mentalizing skills they will need as adults? Byom and Mutlu describe three mechanisms by which humans learn to infer and reason about mental states in social interaction. They identified three components, namely (1) knowledge of the shared context, (2) perception of social cues, and (3) interpretation of actions. [3]

The first TOM mechanism refers to knowledge of the context situated in our common surroundings, also referred to as our shared world knowledge. For instance, in our conversations with others, we try to quickly infer, or guess, what the other person's thoughts, emotions, beliefs, and intentions are so that we can respond adequately. Failure to make the correct inferences may, at the very least, give rise to some abrasive situations.

Consider the situation where Bill and Alice were celebrating their anniversary at a classy restaurant. Bill noticed his wife staring at a man a few tables away. The man slurred his speech and had a boisterous laugh; evidently, he had too much to drink. Bill said, "Do you know that man?" Alice sighed. "He's my ex-husband. He's been drinking like that even when I left him." Bill responded without thinking, "My, that's a long time to be celebrating!"

The anecdote is an oft-narrated joke, but it does illustrate Bill's failure to read Alice's thoughts correctly based on a differently-shared world experience. Was it possible he conflated the context of her ex-husband's jovial inebriation with the event of their wedding anniversary and his own married life? It is possible that Bill was reading Alice's ex-husband's mind more clearly based on shared common experiences. But we digress.

The second mechanism involves perceiving social cues such as recognizing emotions through facial and vocal expressions. Mental states are inherently cognitive events, but we human beings have a broad range of behaviors that manifest our mental states. These include facial expression, eye and vocal cues, physical stances, hand and arm movements, and so forth. Of these, eye or gaze cues is the focus of many scholarly studies on TOM mechanisms. For instance, when people speak to us with an unflinching, direct gaze, we usually take it as a sign of sincerity. In Western cultures, when a speaker averts his gaze, it is a sign that he is speaking sarcastically, and does not believe what he is saying. [4]

The third mechanism is the interpretation of actions, or how humans interact with other humans as well as inanimate objects. We naturally assume that people behave according to their thoughts, beliefs, and intentions. Therefore, by observing how they behave, we gain insight into their mental state.

According to research, children as young as six months old begin to form expectations about such interactions. [5] A favorite game I used to play with my children when they were infants was peek-a-boo. At about this age, babies do not comprehend that you are present when you cover your face, even if you are right in front of them. But when you suddenly uncover your face, they get startled. In time, they come to expect it, and their surprised reaction gives way to a delightful chortle.

As they grow older, children become more observant and get to associate more complex behaviors with their adults' more remote intentions. My two-year-old son Arnold would catch me fixing my hair and powdering my face, and he would roll on the floor bawling in utter despair, "Don't put makeup! Don't go to the office! Stay with me!" My youngest child, Charles, reacted differently when he was the same age. At the sight of me getting dressed, he would ransack his drawers for his outdoor shirt and shorts, his socks and shoes, and climb into the car before I could get in. "I'm coming with you! You can dress me up on the way!"

How about if any of those social cues were absent? Imagine poker players facing each other around a table.

The players try to avoid projecting any emotion or reaction during the game because they could give away their hands (the combination of cards they hold). Successful poker players rely on their ability to bluff convincingly. Therefore, unguarded facial expressions or body movements may be disadvantageous to winning at poker. Thus, the expression "poker face."

The Mechanism Of Linguistic Communication

What is linguistic communication? It is a system of exchanging information using sounds or conventional symbols.

"Linguistic communication involves applying rules that allow people to understand one another even when they do not share the same world vision. Meaning is attributed through a convention that becomes established over time within a given community... Thinking is inseparable from language, which is inseparable from community." – Ludwig Wittgenstein (1889-1951) [6]

Wittgenstein, the Austrian philosopher, believed that in the human mind, thinking and language are inseparable. He explained that we can learn the meaning of a word either within the same language, as when someone uses other words from the language to explain the word to us, or outside the language, as when someone shows us an object to demonstrate what the word is about without using the language. When we learn a new language, then we gain the capacity to understand new ideas and thoughts that do not exist in our own culture. Thus, language helps us express our thoughts and feelings in a way that is meaningful to the community that shares that language.

Sometimes, a language that is shared by two cultures conveys different nuances in each culture. Take the English language, which is spoken both in England and the United States. The anecdote below highlights how two cultures can be separated by a common language.

Seven-year-old Johnny grew up in New Jersey but has British grandparents. On his first solo visit with his grandmother Ellie in Liverpool, Johnny overhears her reassuring his mother over a long-distance phone call. The boy turns wide-eyed when he hears Nana Ellie tell his mom, "Don't worry, dear, I'll make sure to monitor Johnny's screen time. There are too many boobs on the telly. It's such a bad influence!"

On the other hand, there is communication that is non-linguistic or non-verbal. It involves transmitting messages or signals without the use of words, such as through facial expressions, eye contact, objects, gestures, postures, and body language.

Do We Need Language To Think, Or Only To Communicate Completed Thoughts?

The foregoing quote by Wittgenstein states unequivocally that "thinking is inseparable from language."

Notwithstanding this conviction, is it impossible for thinking to occur without language? Then how could babies, who have not yet learned to talk, think, which they do at some fundamental level? Extending further backward in our history, when primitive homo sapiens had not yet developed even basic language forms, were they not thinking? When the first early human learned to use fire, which most likely preceded the use of language, was this not the product of thinking?

As a mother, I knew when my newborn child was hungry because he cried. He was contented because he slept peacefully. He was happy when he played. And when he was irritated, he cried a different way. This is basic communication, which reflects fundamental thinking. Even without language, a rudimentary form of communication exists which shows that primary thought processes are taking place.

This does not necessarily contradict Wittgenstein; rather, it qualifies his ideas. Thinking at a high level, whereby we develop broad and profound concepts, is necessarily dependent on language because it requires abstraction and analysis. Verbal language is structured and governed by sets of rules which help us organize our thoughts and make logical analyses. But the more basic feelings and impulses, which are forms of thought processes, exist without language.

There is a segment of our population who do not have the facility of language because of some mental impediment. For instance, people with extreme autism have no speech ability. While they are unable to express their feelings through spoken language, they still have five senses through which they connect with the outside world. They can absorb sensations of color, smell, music, numbers, and movement. Might they not convey their thoughts using these media, which do not require language? It may be argued that these are non-linguistic forms of expression by which those unable to speak can communicate. [7]

While communication and thinking can take place without language, the level and manner of thinking are nevertheless shaped by language, and language characteristics are determined by the civilization that developed it. Fundamental thinking can take place without language, but abstract thinking can only be fostered by a well-developed system of linguistic communication.

The Mechanism Of Brain Functionality

What distinguishes human beings physiologically from other animals? Certainly not our development at birth, since many other animals are ready to walk and run a few hours after birth. Many other animals are stronger than us and are better adapted to their environments. But we have to develop by another twenty years after birth before we can function adequately in society.

Physiologically, what we have over and above other creatures is our brain. Humans have the largest brain in proportion to their body size compared to other living creatures. Our brains are also the most complex, having developed specialized regions that have distinctive structures and functions. [8] The following is a simplified diagram of the brain showing some of the more important regions.

Cerebral Cortex [9]

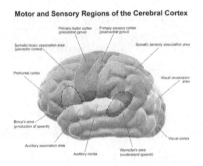

Motor and Sensory Regions of the Cerebral Cortex

How do these different systems figure in our mental processes? The term for the phenomenon that enables the brain to categorize, memorize, and retrieve information is brain plasticity, which is "the ability of the nervous system to change its activity in response to intrinsic or extrinsic stimuli by reorganizing its structure, functions, or connections."[10] The term comes from the Greek term *plastikos* meaning "molded" or "formed."

How Information Is Categorized

Categorization is the ability to group items and events into functional categories. It is a fundamental trait of sophisticated thought. The ability of the brain to categorize information involves many neural systems such as the following (bear with us, this will involve some difficult words, but focus on their functions). In categorization and classification tasks, the subject is exposed to the sensory stimuli (for example, visual stimuli), differentiates it from other stimuli, and decides for each stimulus which category or group it belongs.

Academic studies [11,12,13] have confirmed that there is no single "categorization area" in the brain, in the same way that there is a visual, auditory, motor, or sensory area. Categories are represented in a distributed manner throughout the brain by involving multiple neural systems. The multiple memory systems framework comprises many of the systems involved in categorization. Multiple systems may be called to solve categorization problems since categorization tasks are not process-pure (i.e., dedicated purely to categorization). [14]

1. Neocortical regions

The neocortex is the largest part of the cerebral cortex, comprising almost half of the volume of the human brain. Neurologists believe that it is responsible for higher-order brain functions, including cognition, sensory perception, generation of motor commands, spatial reasoning, language, decision-making, and other emotive-cognitive processes. [15]

1.1 Sensory modalities (visual, auditory, somatosensory, olfactory, etc.) - These relay the outside stimuli into our brains, as well as encode that information into our long-term memory. Visual corresponds to sight, auditory to sound, somatosensory to localized sensations such as pressure, pain, or warmth, and olfactory to smell.

1.2 Prefrontal cortex (PFC) – The PFC occupies a greater proportion of the human cerebral cortex than it does in animals, suggesting that it likely contributes to the cognitive capacities that distinguish humans from animals. Experience more readily modifies the PFC than it does the sensory cortex. PFC neurons reflect abstract rule-based categorical distinctions. [16]

1.3 Parietal Cortex (PC) – The PC seems to highlight visuospatial functions and link information from the perceptual system (stimulated by sensory information) with the potentially appropriate response. Visuospatial functions involve identifying visual and spatial relationships among objects. Visuospatial ability is measured by the degree to which a person is able "to imagine objects, to make global shapes by locating small components, or to understand the differences and similarities between objects." [17]

1.4 Premotor and motor cortex (PMC and MC) – These regions are located within the frontal lobe. The PMC is involved in selecting the appropriate plan for voluntary movements. On the other hand, the MC appears to be involved in the execution of these planned voluntary movements. [18] Categorical decision tasks involve the PMC and MC in selecting and executing an appropriate behavior. Category learning can result in plasticity in brain systems, such that reliance on motor systems increases as expertise on the behavior learned is developed and reliance on other systems decreases. When humans perform familiar rather than novel classifications, there are stronger signals in the PMC rather than in the prefrontal cortex, and vice versa.

2. The hippocampus and the medial temporal lobes

The hippocampus is the part of the brain that plays a major role in learning and memory. It is a complex brain structure embedded deep in the temporal lobe. It is also "a plastic and vulnerable structure that gets damaged by a variety of stimuli." [19] The hippocampus has long been acknowledged to play an important role in remembering details of specific experiences. Recently, its role in integrating information across events to generalize knowledge has been recognized. [20] One type of generalization that the hippocampus enables, known as episodic inference, allows the memory of past and current events to be combined such that knowledge from both episodes can be combined – i.e., that they form a category.

The medial temporal lobes (MTL) are anatomically and functionally connected with the cortex and appear to be specialized for rapid learning of individual instances. [21]

Some studies are not certain about the role of the MTL in category learning. [22] However, one potential contribution of this region of the brain follows from the observation made by researchers that the information acquired from it can be transferred to new situations, thus aiding in grouping different bits of information under a common category. If a stimulus (for example, guitar music) is in two categories (classical and modern), then another stimulus (piano music) that is in one category (classical) might also be in the other category (modern), this categorization task involves the MTL. [23]

3. The basal ganglia and corticostriatal loops

The basal ganglia are a group of nuclei located below the cortex (i.e., subcortical nuclei) comprising the striatum, globus pallidus, substantia nigra, and subthalamic nucleus in humans. [24] The following diagram gives us a picture of the basal ganglia. The categorization tasks that involve this area of the brain are:

- *Trial and error prototype learning* (stimuli are formed as distortions of a prototype stimulus),
- *Information integration learning* (stimuli are grouped based on an abstract feature),
- *Probabilistic classification* (multiple-independent features are correlated to identify membership in a particular category), and
- *Arbitrary categorization tasks* (stimuli in each group do not share any identifiable common

characteristics, thus the category membership of each must be independently learned). [25]

Structure Of The Basal Ganglia With The Thalamus [26]

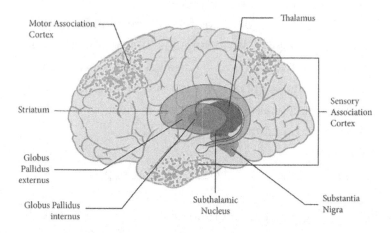

The primary role of the basal ganglia is to interact with the sensory modalities (visual, auditory, somatosensory, olfactory, etc.) in the cortex to process the information triggered by the stimuli. The basal ganglia then aid in the generalization of this information, which is an important step in categorization. Neuroscientists hypothesize that generalization is achieved by the merging of cortical information onto the striatum, as well as other intricate mechanisms involving parts of the basal ganglia. [27]

We must keep in mind that while the diagram shows what appear to be independent structures, the basal ganglia is not isolated from the rest of the brain. They are closely connected with the cerebral cortex as well as other subcortical regions (areas under the cortex) and participate in multiple-independent neural networks known as corticostriatal loops, shown in the next diagram. These loops are regulatory circuits of the brain that link the cortex with the regions beneath it, the basal ganglia included. They filter and selectively identify stimuli on which the brain bases its cognitive and behavioral responses. [28]

Corticostriatal Loops [29]

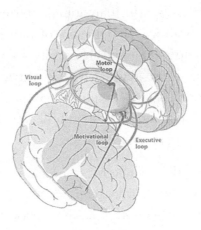

The role of the corticostriatal loops is to maintain separation among different types of stimuli and have specialized functions. The visual corticostriatal loop plays a role in visual stimulus processing. The motor corticostriatal loop is involved in response selection. Finally, the executive and motivational loops perform tasks in processing feedback and reward. [30]

4. The midbrain dopaminergic system and reinforcement learning mechanisms

Dopamine is a type of neurotransmitter made in our bodies that makes us feel good. Our nervous system uses dopamine to send messages between nerve cells, which is what a neurotransmitter is – a chemical messenger. [31] Dopamine enables us to feel pleasure, satisfaction, and motivation. When we feel good because we succeeded in something, the feeling is due to a surge of dopamine in the brain. [32]

Reinforcement learning (RL), on the other hand, is an "adaptive process by which an animal utilizes its previous experience to improve the outcomes of future choices." [33] Under RL theory, an animal chooses its actions according to how much future reward it may expect from each action. This implies that computational theory provides a useful model for understanding how much reward is expected based on past experiences.

The midbrain dopaminergic, or dopamine, area (DA) plays an important role in reinforcement learning. The activity of the DA neurons (i.e., the release of dopamine upon encountering a pleasurable stimulus) provides a mechanism that modifies synapses. (Synapses are the spaces between neurons. They are more thoroughly described in the next section.) Synaptic modifications, in turn, create the mechanisms for memory and learning. It enables a particular class of reinforcement learning mechanisms that underlie much of human and animal behavior. [34]

Supposing you visit a beach resort for the first time. You find the experience entirely enjoyable – taking in the sun and surf, lazing cozily on the white sand, relaxing to music, and dining on fresh seafood and cool drinks prepared to perfection. Your brain's sensory modalities relay messages to the other regions of your brain. The DA releases dopamines that trigger changes in your synapses with memories of the reward you experience, and your learning is reinforced that you would want to visit this place again in the future. On the other hand, if you found the experience disappointing – the place was dirty, accommodations were poor, the food was bland – then the lack of pleasure results in the absence of a reward and, therefore, negative reinforcement learning. You can rest assured you will never make any plans to revisit the place.

Many other structures support the DA. For instance, a part of the brain known as the ventral tegmental area (VTA) is well known for regulating reward consumption, memory, learning, and addiction behaviors by moderating the release of dopamine in the downstream regions. [35]

How Information Is Stored

We store information in our brains as memories, the building blocks of the brain. Memory is defined as "the process in which the mind interprets, stores, and retrieves information." [36] Everything important that we learn, we commit to memory, especially the lessons that help keep us safe (like accidents or injuries from handling sharp or hot objects). Our fondest memories also include treasured memories that shape our identities and cherished life stories.

Synapses

We mentioned synapses in our discussion about the dopaminergic area and reinforcement learning. When something we learn is reinforced, we store that information in the form of memories. How our brain stores and retrieves memories is fascinating because, with each new memory, the human brain reshapes itself. This phenomenon involves those parts of the brain's structure known as synapses. Synapses are tiny gaps between the brain cells, as shown in the magnified diagram below.

The Synapse [37]

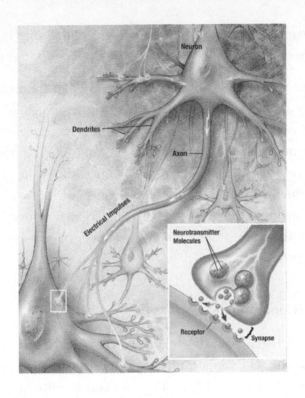

Brain cells, also called neurons, communicate with each other through the workings of a sophisticated electrochemical system. When a memory is made, the electrical charge of one cell undergoes a change that triggers the release of neurotransmitters (chemicals) across the synapses. The neuron on the other side of the synapse then senses the neurotransmitters that were released, causing the receiving neuron to trigger electrical charges. The memories are encoded in the circuits connecting these brain cells, and the synapses provide the means for these circuit connections. Each new memory creates a new circuit where it is encoded, and that is how the brain changes.

When a memory is frequently encountered, the neurons that comprise the circuit are frequently stimulated and their connection becomes stronger, making it easier for these neurons to stimulate each other in time. But when a memory is seldom revisited, the connection in the circuit encoding it weakens, until communication between the neurons stops altogether. The brain stores memories best when the connections linking networks of neurons are strengthened.

The Hippocampus

Several regions of the brain are responsible for storing memories. The hippocampus is comprised of two regions located deep in the brain. They are curled in the shape of seahorses, as shown in the following diagram. The paired regions are vital for initial memory formation and for converting short-term to long-term memories. In the latter process, the hippocampus retrieves information from the working (short-term) memory regions and changes the brain's physical neural wiring in the manner described earlier. [38] The new connections created between synapses and neurons remain as long as they are useful and thus comprise long-term memory.

The Hippocampus [39] : Locations In The Brain And Its Similarity To A Seahorse [40]

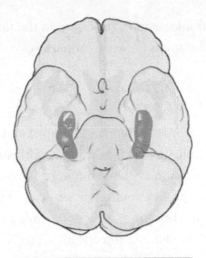

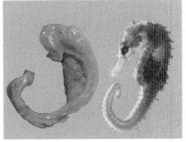

The Amygdala

The amygdala is another important region that plays a role in storing memories. It is an almond-shaped region of the brain that helps process emotions. [41] Emotional arousal stimulates the amygdala, resulting in the modulation of memory storage situated in other regions of the brain. Amygdala activation intensifies memory consolidation by promoting neural plasticity (remember, the ability of neurons to adjust their activity and structure) and information processes in the target regions, thereby altering brain network properties. [42]

Action Steps

This chapter includes a long and complicated explanation of how the brain undertakes the categorization task. To recall, categorization is the grouping of items according to similar traits they mutually possess. The scientific explanation of this brain function cannot avoid some concepts that are difficult to capture verbally. Majority of us learn better if we view images like the one below.

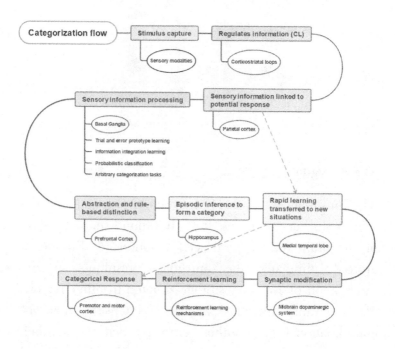

The mind map above is a pictured explanation of the categorization task explained in this chapter. Look at it and see if you understand this better than the worded explanation. Then go back to the section "How information is categorized" and try reading the salient parts of it with the above mind map in view. Does it make more sense than the first time you read the section?

Moving On

The categorization flow mind map should appear simpler to understand than the written discussion, but it still leaves much to be explained. You will find the interpretation of the mind map and the detailed process of its creation explained in Chapter 8, using the information in the categorization section in Chapter 2. For now, however, there are a few things about mind maps that we will need to learn, beginning with the next chapter.

Key Takeaways

1. The Theory of Mind refers to our ability to accurately understand other people's mental states. There are three mechanisms of TOM: a shared world knowledge, perception of social cues, and the interpretation of actions.
2. Linguistic communication is a system of exchanging information using sounds or conventional symbols. Language is a requisite for

high-level thinking, although at a more fundamental level, thoughts and communication may take place without the use of words.

3. Brain functionality is governed by the interactions of areas of the brain that carry out both specialized and overlapping roles.

4. The categorization mechanism involves the neocortical regions including the sensory modalities, prefrontal cortex, the parietal cortex, and the premotor and motor cortex; the medial temporal lobe including the hippocampi; the basal ganglia and corticostriatal loops; and the dopaminergic system.

5. Memory storage and recall involve the synapses, the hippocampi, and the amygdala. These functions are not exclusive to the regions but rather are redundant and overlapping.

3

MASTERING MEMORY

HOW YOU CAN USE MEMORY VISUALIZATION TECHNIQUES AND TAKE ADVANTAGE OF YOUR MEMORY PALACE IN REAL LIFE

E veryone who is a fan of television quiz shows likely knows *Jeopardy!* Contestants select categories under which are clues in the form of answers. They then provide the appropriate response to each clue in the form of a question. Setting aside the mandatory question form, here are some of the sample clues. [1] Let's have two per category. Write down your answers to the questions (let's have two per category):

Category: Theater, Plays, and Folklore

Question 1: In 1965, at age 20, Helen Mirren played this Egyptian at the Old Vic.

Question 2: The four words that complete the line from "Jack and the Beanstalk," "Fee, fi, fo, fum, I smell the…"

Category: Sports

Question 1: In 2014, 2015, and 2019, Novak Djokovic defeated this Swiss player in the Wimbledon final.

Question 2: Also a term in baseball, it's what the British call a soccer field.

Category: History

Question 1: The Sixth Amendment grants the right to a speedy and public this.

Question 2: In 1959, she became president of India's Congress Party and joined Parliament five years later.

Alright, pens down and check your answers against the correct answers at the end of this chapter. How many did you score right? If you got at least half right, then you are either a wide reader with a good memory, or you're at least 50 years old.

Yes, I chose the questions that I could answer on sight. I'm not a person with an exceptional memory or IQ, it just happens that I lived through the period when Helen Mirren was a young stage actress and India had her first and only female prime minister. Younger readers who remember their rhymes, like sports, and studied civics lessons well would likely answer the rest correctly, but not these two dated questions at face value, unless they are wide readers who can memorize well.

Having an exceptional memory is a divine gift that a rare few are endowed with. For the rest of us plain mortals, there is still hope because memorizing is an active creative process that can be developed. Before we can successfully develop our memory skills, it helps to understand the principles that govern memorization. There are ten of them.

<u>The Ten Memory Principles</u> [2]

1. Interest – Learning is more effective if you have a reason to remember it. Develop a personal and active interest in what we are studying.

2. Intent to remember – Form a positive attitude that you will remember the information. Concentrate, take notes, pay close attention, and avoid drifting off.

3. Basic background – Remembering becomes easier if you have a strong foundation on the subject.

4. Selectivity – Nobody can remember everything about everything, so be selective about what you want to commit to memory. Decide what is most important to you, and from that pool of knowledge, select the parts that you want to study and learn well.

5. Meaningful organization – If you group your thoughts into categories that are meaningful to you, the material will be easier for you to understand and learn. Alphabetizing, mnemonics, chronological arrangement, and other such memory tools may prove helpful.

6. Recitation – Verbalizing the material aloud in your own words is a powerful tool for transferring information from short-term to long-term memory. After reading a portion of the material, pause and recite what the lesson means in your own statements.

7. Mental visualization – Make a mental picture of the thoughts you want to remember. Visualizing allows a more holistic engagement of your brain, beyond the involvement achieved through reading and listening alone. With visualization, you are able to trigger more synapses in multiple parts of the brain and activate more circuits.

8. Association – When new information is associated with thoughts already familiar to you, memory is increased. The material you previously learned and recall that you can link to new concepts enlarges your "brain file." The result is that you remember the new information better and faster.

9. Consolidation – Your brain does not fully absorb all the new knowledge instantly; therefore, you must allow enough time for new information to soak in. Let the new information "marinate" in your mind by writing notes, devising memory aids, taking practice tests, and other techniques.

10. Distributed practice – To make your learning more effective, it is better to schedule a series of shorter study sessions distributed over several days rather than having fewer but longer compressed study sessions. Time your study periods so that after every hour of study, afford yourself a ten-minute break. Allocate a schedule for each subject and review your material repeatedly and frequently.

The memory principles provide the cornerstone for many of the memorization techniques that have been developed and refined to guide students, workers, parents, managers, bus drivers, pilots, nuclear plant operators, astronauts, and practically anybody who must rely on their memory to perform well. The following are some of these memory-enhancing methods.

SEE Principle (Senses-Exaggeration-Energize)

The SEE memory technique is built on the principle that something from our external environment can be remembered by employing our sensory perception, exaggerating what we perceived, and energizing the memory with action or animation. The key is to make the memory vivid and interesting to the point that it becomes difficult to forget.

The SEE technique is an effective method to use when trying to remember faces and names. This was a challenge for me as a professor at the start of every semester. Handling four or five classes with anywhere from thirty to fifty students meant that I had to (or at least try my best to) remember as many as 250 students, many of them new to me. After the first few years of teaching, I was able to develop a system that was largely based on the SEE technique. First, I look at the student to find a distinguishing characteristic. A mole on the face, multiple ear piercings, and arm tattoos (although they were against the dress code). Most of the time, the feature is something that I may only have perceived, like seemingly large eyes.

The next step was to exaggerate the feature. The mole could appear to occupy half the face, the arm tattoos may look more colorful or dramatic, the ear-piercing studs may seem to weigh the ear down, and the eyes may look like they are protruding from the face. Then, I picture the exaggerated feature relative to the student's name. Bob had the large mole, so the large round mole would fit in the letter O in BOB's name. Gemma is the girl with the heavy ear studs that look like gems. Mark with the tattoos had "marks" all over his body. Ivan has large eyes, so I picture his name as EYE-van. The more ridiculous the image and link, the better animated or dynamic the memory.

The Link Method

Notice how the SEE technique involved associating things with each other? In the example, students' physical features were linked to exaggerated images and then to their names. This is one way of applying a more generic memorization method known as the link method. It makes memorization effective by linking new material (short-term memory) with concepts already known and familiar (long-term memory).

A frequent use of the link method is learning a new variation of something you are already familiar with. For instance, many like me who are not culinary-savvy have difficulty remembering recipes. Once, when I wanted to make pasta carbonara for my children, I looked up the recipe online and noticed how the sauce for carbonara was very similar to that of the chicken ala king we learned in high school. For the new recipe, I just needed to substitute a few ingredients from the old recipe. Thus, something new was learned by relating it to previous knowledge.

The link method is based on the association principle; it is easier to learn something new if you connect the new information to something you already know well.

The Loci Method

As I was growing up, my mother drilled into our minds that "everything has a place, and everything should be in its own place." We had a designated place for studying, which was in our family library (really, just a quiet room in my Dad's home office with a long table, good lighting and air-conditioning, and a collection of general reference books). She believed that providing a place conducive to concentration and learning would help us study better and get good grades. Recent studies suggest, however, that such is not always the case.

Robert A. Bjork, a distinguished research professor of psychology, is known for his classic studies about the effect of location and learning. In a 1978 experiment, students comprising a test group were made to study a list of 40 vocabulary words in two different rooms – one cluttered and windowless, and the other well-kept with a view of a courtyard. This group performed better on a test compared to the control group of students who studied the words twice in the same room. [3]

What accounts for this outcome? Scientists say that the brain makes subtle connections between what it is learning and the background sensations it is exposed to at the time, whether it is aware of such sensations or not. It is likely that when the brain is forced to make multiple associations as it absorbs the new material, it affords more neural anchors to the information being learned. The varied external context enriches the information and slows down the process of forgetting. [4]

The specific association of location and learning is also called the Method of Loci (MOL), from the word loci which is the Latin word for locations or places. A systematic application of the MOL is the Memory Palace. Let's learn more about it.

The Memory Palace Method

A special type of MOL is the Memory Palace technique, "a memorization strategy, based on visualizations of familiar spatial environments to recall information," [5] Memory Palace involves visualizing a location or physical space we are familiar with. We then link terms, facts, or concepts that we are memorizing to spots in this location. If the attachment is successful, our brain will easily remember and recall the spaces and the terms associated with them.

How The Memory Palace Method Began

The beginning of the Memory Palace/MOL is haunting yet historic. Its origin is attributed to a 5th-century BCE Greek poet, Simonides, who was invited to sing at a banquet in Thessaly. The banquet's host, Scotus, hired the poet to sing a victory ode to the triumphant boxer being honored by the feast, but while Simonides praised the guest of honor, he included boxing demigods Castor and Pollux. The digression irked Scotus, who thereafter paid Simonides only half the promised fee, instructing him to collect the remainder from the two mythological beings he had praised so highly.

After he returned to the banquet, a servant delivered a message to Simonides that two young men waited outside to speak with him. The poet went out to the street but did not find his purported visitors there. As he looked around for them, the roof of the banquet hall he had just left suddenly collapsed together with the entire building. Everyone inside was killed. Legend has it that the two men who called out Simonides and disappeared were Castor and Pollux, who spared Simonides's life because he praised them.

Simonides then helped the authorities to identify the bodies, which were so disfigured because the structure obliterated all beneath it. Since Simonides was the only person in the banquet to survive, he retained a unique mental picture of the seating arrangements of the participants. He, therefore, recalled the name of each person at the banquet based on their location around the table and placed the names to bodies to identify the victims and facilitate the necessary funeral rites. This was the first known use of the memory palace, which Simonides later developed and extended as a memory tool. [6] It was thereafter adopted and extensively used in ancient Greek and Roman classical written works, up until the invention and use of the printing press. [7]

Performing The Memory Palace Technique

How does a Memory Palace work? The University of Pittsburgh suggests the following steps: [8]

<u>Step 1:</u> Identify your memory palace. It should be a place that you know very well, such as a place you lived, studied, worked in, or visited. It can even be an open park or places in a movie whose scenes you know by heart. Close your eyes and mentally move through the spaces of your palace, naming exactly what you see. Do the following:

1.1. List different places that you think will make good memory palaces. This will comprise your collection of different information pools (for example, subjects or courses).

1.2. Draw a floor plan or map for each memory palace.

1.3. Form a linear journey through the palace that does not have a dead end.

<u>Step 2:</u> List the distinctive objects, features, stations, or

points in your palace, each of which becomes a memory slot.

<u>Step 3:</u> Associate memory slots with information you want to memorize.

<u>Step 4:</u> Take a memory walk through your palace.

The result should be that you will be better able to recall material you committed to memory as you mentally access the different parts of the palace with which you associated them. Let's illustrate this with a simple example.

Example Of A Memory Palace

Let's say you are the hands-on manager of an enterprise, a business whose every aspect you run. You would like to remember as much as you can about your business to be better able to make effective decisions. Let's say you choose your house as your memory palace.

Begin by summoning up in your mind a picture of your house – either the house you lived in growing up or the one you live in now, whichever to you is more memorable. As you walk through your house, you see several of the most important areas: bedroom, bathroom, kitchen, living room, and study.

Now, identify the important elements of your business that you wish to monitor. A good list would include marketing, finance, operations, human resources, and strategic planning. These are the topics for which you will need memory slots to store the individual facts, ideas, and concepts that pertain to the topic area. You may associate the living room with marketing, the kitchen with operations and production, the study with strategic planning, the bathroom with finance, and the bedroom with human resources.

Plan a linear route that passes through all the places in your palace. The order is up to you; it may be a logical or chronological order, but it must be meaningful to you. Your business ought to logically be anchored on your market, so you could start in the living room. Proceed to strategic planning (the study), operations and production (the kitchen), and on to finance (the bathroom). Finally, visit human resources (the bedroom) before you return to the living room. You could modify this order, based on your preference.

In each room, list the possible memory slots. In the kitchen, these may consist of the refrigerator, the freezer, the microwave, the condiments shelf, the utensils, drawers, pots and pans, and so forth. Then associate each memory slot with information you want to memorize. In the operations and production field, these could be logistics details, raw materials inventory, production processes, finished goods packaging, cost calculations, prototype design, and other concepts you wish to commit to memory. The more meaningful the association is to you, the better able you will be at recalling the information later.

After populating your memory palace, take frequent walk-throughs around it. Repetition is essential in enhancing faster and more accurate recall, so frequently revisiting parts of the palace is essential not only to remember what was learned but to keep them updated.

The Peg System

A different but related method of memorizing is called the peg system, also referred to as the mnemonic peg system. This method works by creating one-on-one mental associations between two objects or ideas. Henry Herdson invented it in the 1600s. [9] The mnemonic peg system is a useful device for remembering a list of items in order, such as when the items are ranked in order of importance or chronology.

There are several variations of this method, one of which is the rhyming mnemonic peg method. A popular version rhymes peg words with numbers, and the ranked items are matched with the corresponding peg. The following table will give you an idea of the linking process.

A Memory Peg Table

Order	Memory Peg	Item on list	Image
One	Sun	Rice	Rice stalks swaying in the glaring sun
Two	Shoe	Beef	A shoe with bull horns and ears in front and a tail behind
Three	Tree	Chicken	Chickens roosting on a tree
Four	Door	Pork	A pig standing upright opening the door
Five	Hive	Honey	Honey dripping from a hive
Six	Sticks	Cheese	Cheese fashioned as sticks

Seven	Heaven	Bread	Bread raining down like mana from heaven
Eight	Gate	Fruits	Fruits hanging on the gate
Nine	Vine	Veggies	Vegetables hanging on a vine
Ten	Pen	Eggs	Eggs with faces drawn by a Sharpie pen

The memory peg technique, in essence, follows the SEE principle. The memory pegs are chosen based on how they rhyme with the order number, and how readily they can call to mind an image, much as the visual sensory step in SEE. Objects make the best memory pegs because abstract words are more difficult to draw images for – but then, the choice is best left to the person devising the system. In the table, the rhyming pegs are easily visualized; one-sun, two-shoe, and so forth.

Next is to "hang" the item on the peg. We do this by creating a fun visual image that will instantly trigger the memory. Rice stalks swaying in the glaring sun could be the first image. A shoe with bull horns and a tail could be the second. Write down the images on the third table to serve as your memory code. The more exaggerated the association, the better the memory peg.

Finally, in the third step, akin to the "energize" phase, add some actions that lead from one peg to the next, in the order they were written. The rice stalks swaying in the glaring sun break off and fall to the ground. They become shoes with horns and tails and walk to the tree to join the chickens. The chickens fall from the branches as the tree splits open to reveal a door that is opened by a pig standing upright. And so on. The narrative created is another memory technique that keeps the pegs in their order of enumeration.

The presence of a storyline or narrative is a powerful memory tool that keeps things in order. Another such tool is the journey method, where the pegs are organized according to the sequence in which they are encountered on a mental journey.

The Journey Method

The Journey Method is a technique of remembering lists of objects or items by visualizing images about them at points along a journey we are familiar with. It is an ancient method that is also termed the "mental walk" technique, and it is closely related to the MOL technique attributed to Simonides of Ceos in 477 BCE. [10]

Oftentimes, we visit places from our past and suddenly recall events, people, or ideas that were closely related to those places. Couples married for decades would spend their vacations, maybe celebrate anniversaries, in places that were meaningful to them, such as their honeymoon resort or the romantic bistro where she accepted his proposal. Long-term memories are triggered by the journeys we take or places we visit.

Conversely, we can also use journeys to help us recall our short-term memories if we exert a conscious effort to make the associations. Recalling the stops along a road trip enables us to remember the meals we took and the people we met along the way. The side trips and scheduled activities we undertake when we go to other countries for a seminar or conference can help us retain and recall much of the substance of that seminar or conference.

Using the journey technique systematically can enhance its effectiveness. Before embarking on the journey, prepare for it by identifying the landmarks in your mind for you to "store" new information. If you have at least ten landmarks, write them down in the order that you expect to encounter them. Remember this sequence every time you use this particular journey for memory recall.

Then, if you are trying to remember a list, pick an image to represent each item on your list. If the item is something that can be "seen" objectively, such as people or things, then identifying an image would be simple and immediate. If the item is virtual or an abstract concept, then creating an image would be more complicated and you may have to use "image clues." In any case, it is a good idea to exaggerate these images (as in the SEE technique) to make them more memorable. [11]

Action Steps

In the section "The Peg System," we constructed a memory peg table that used words rhyming with the numbers that corresponded to the order of the memory peg. A mnemonic system can also be created out of memory pegs associated with the letters of the alphabet. You could also select the class of items that comprise the memory pegs – for instance, land animals beginning with the letter that stood for the order on the list. You can create a list of no more than 26 items to remember with this system. To illustrate, let's assume the items are your grocery list, and the first item is "celery." The resulting memory peg table will look something like this:

Order	Memory Peg	Item on list	Image
A	Aardvark	Celery	Aardvark with celery coming out of its ears.
B	Bear	...	...
C	Camel		
D	Deer		
E	Elephant		
F	...		
...			

Of course, you could imagine an aardvark eating celery. However, since a grocery list will include many food items, picturing animals eating different types of food may not be memorable enough for the mnemonic system to work. An aardvark is an animal with large ears, so the image will probably be more striking if you picture celery stalks coming out of its ears.

Try completing the table above, or you could create your own list (not necessarily a grocery list) that would be more relevant to you. You could also substitute the suggested animals with those you are more familiar with. Use whatever pegs, items, or images work best for you. Then see if the images you come up with help you remember the items on your list. Don't forget to come up with a story linking the images to each other. A little practice will go a long way in making this system work.

Moving On

Many memory-enhancing techniques have been devised over the years. This chapter only describes a few of the more popular ones. Many others have come up with methods known only to them, which is fine for as long as they work. The same mental processes involved in memory enhancement are likewise employed in mind mapping, as the next chapter shows.

Key Takeaways

1. Memory principles that provide the foundation for memorization techniques include interest, the intent to remember, basic background, selectivity, meaningful organization, recitation, mental visualization, association, consolidation, and distributed practice.

2. The Senses-Exaggeration-Energize (SEE) Memory Technique involves employing sensory perception, exaggerating the perception, and energizing the memory to make the memory so vivid as to be difficult to forget.

3. The Link Method associates new material in short-term memory with previous knowledge in long-term memory. It is the general category of memory techniques under which the SEE technique falls.

4. The Method of Loci (MOL) involves relating memory to a specific location. The Memory Palace is a sophisticated memory system categorized as a loci technique.

5. The Mnemonic Peg System involves creating one-on-one associations between two objects or ideas.

6. The Journey Method is an MOL technique that memorizes lists of objects by visualizing images about them at familiar points along a journey.

Answers to the game at the beginning of the chapter:

Category: Theater, Plays, and Folklore

Answer 1: Cleopatra

Answer 2: "Blood of an Englishman."

Category: Sports

Answer 1: Roger Federer

Answer 2: A pitch.

Category: History

Answer 1: Trial

Answer 2: Indira Gandhi

4

OVERCOMING MIND MAP CHALLENGES

HOW TO EXPLOIT MIND MAP'S ADVANTAGES AND CONQUER ITS DISADVANTAGES FOR CRITICAL THINKING

"A lion chased me up a tree, and I greatly enjoyed the view from the top." - Confucius [1]

In the 1960s, the post-war economy made people more prosperous at about the same time technology made cars cheaper to manufacture. The result? More families flocking to cities and buying more cars than the cities planned for. My father, driving our Buick LeSabre through the streets downtown, would unwittingly get us mired in hours-long gridlocks. It was not his fault, of course; sometimes it's just bad luck that we would turn down a street only to find ourselves stuck in stand-still traffic with no opportunity to turn away or back out.

During times like, these, Dad would light-heartedly joke, "I wish someone could invent the flying camera that we could send up to take pictures of the roads we would be passing through before we get into them. That way, we could avoid the congested streets." Then we would all chuckle at the absurdity of the idea.

Dad could have put Nostradamus to shame. Today, commercial Global Positioning System (GPS) devices are widely used. With eye-in-the-sky accuracy, a screen shows you where the car is headed and the conditions of the roads surrounding it. A charming female voice alerts you that you should prepare to make a turn soon. It even warns you when a traffic enforcer is nearby. Everything that Dad wanted, and more.

In retrospect, wishing to be guided by a view from above as you travel down uncertain roads is simply common sense. In a car, your two-dimensional view limits your ability to make good decisions about where to go. Your vision is constrained by unnecessary details of things close by, and you have no perspective regarding your desired destination. But imagine traveling by helicopter – say, to broadcast the morning news traffic advisory. Your view of the same roads from above expands tremendously to pick up details such as obstructions and alternate routes on the way to your destination. With one glance, you understand the entire picture to better guide the earthbound travelers below.

Mind maps provide us with the same perspective from above and allow us to view the entire concept in its spatial layout. A mind map has the main subject at the center, major themes about the subject as branches radiating from the center, and details about the themes as twigs shooting out from the branches. You can create an unlimited number of associations and connections visibly linked to the main idea.

As we shall later see, mind maps come in many forms. But whatever the form, all mind maps have five essential characteristics: [2]

1. Attention is immediately drawn to the main subject by locating it at the center of the diagram.

2. Major themes about the subject are formed as branches radiating from the center.

3. Each branch corresponds to a keyword or image printed or drawn along its line.

4. Less important topics emanate as "twigs" out of their relevant branches.

5. The branches comprise a connected nodal structure where ideas are joined to each other. Branches closer to the center are of greater importance, while nodes and twigs on the periphery correspond to the less important details.

Recall the Tennis Mind Map featured in Chapter 1. The main subject, major topics, branches, twigs, nodes, and their keywords are readily identifiable at first sight. At once, you gain a sense of the relationships between the topics and the progression of their hierarchy, from the broader subjects to the minor details through the branches, nodes, and twigs. How skillfully we structure these elements defines how effectively we use mind maps as a tool.

The characteristics of mind maps described above create both advantages and disadvantages in using this tool. Some advantages of using mind maps include the following:

- *Compatibility with the brain*
- *Providing balance with the brain*
- *The use of keywords*
- *Simplifying complicated examples*
- *Enhancing creativity*
- *Quicker note-taking and review*
- *Employing special mnemonics*

Compatibility With The Brain

Mind mapping is an efficient tool for getting information in and out of your brain quickly because its construction mimics how the brain thinks. The brain links new information with information stored in long-term memory, expanding knowledge by creating multiple pathways through its 86 billion neurons.

The Similarity Between Brain Cells And Mind Maps

Brain Cell (Neuron) [3]

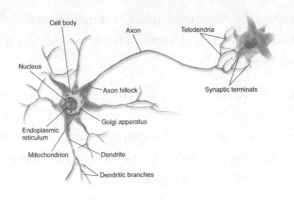

Mind Map [4]

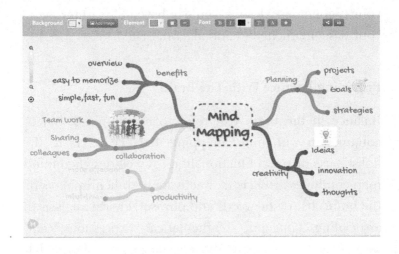

A mind map operates much like a random-access memory device (RAM) sources information, compared with a sequential access storage device. We can liken this distinction to many of our electronic devices. Sequential access involves reading through files stored one after the other before you reach the information you want, such as data stored on magnetic tape. Random access involves immediately reaching information without having to read through other files first.

Millennials will remember watching their favorite videos or music on both tapes and compact discs. The tapes are sequential access devices requiring you to fast-forward and rewind the tape to find a point midway between the beginning and end. Compact discs, on the other hand, only require you to select the track you want and play it without going through the other tracks. Imagine if our brain worked sequentially, like magnetic tape. To recall your trigonometry lesson, you will have to "read through" your basic mathematics and algebra first!

Providing Balance With The Brain

Balance in the brain can refer to many things, but in conjunction with mind mapping, balance refers to the holistic use of brain functionalities. A well-designed mind map combines artifacts that activate both hemispheres of the brain. Its use of words and phrases, logical analysis in associating concepts, mathematical expressions, and similar devices employ the specializations of the left hemisphere, while drawings, pictures, colors, and their spatial and creative organization on the diagram employ the specializations of the right hemisphere. Students inclined toward artistic and collaborative activities performed better academically at all levels when they used mind maps as a principal learning tool. [5] Arab students positively responded to the use of mind mapping and found the method beneficial in learning English. [6]

The Use Of Keywords

Other note-taking devices use many, and frequently unnecessary, words to convey meaning. They try to lay out in verbal explanations what the brain already knows intuitively. Mind mapping does away with verbiage and focuses on keywords that label its branches and twigs. The brain latches onto the keywords that evoke long-term memory concepts.

Because mind maps eliminate the need for linguistic rules such as grammar and syntax, it becomes an effective tool to communicate concepts across different languages. Understanding keywords in another language and comprehending their relationships through a mind map foregoes the need for students to master fluency in that language before they can study subjects couched in it. Mind mapping was found to be a useful strategy for teaching English-based general education sciences classes for Arabic speakers in the United Arab Emirates. [7] Nursing students in Egypt likewise found mind mapping superior to other conventional study methods, particularly in overcoming issues with retention and recall. [8]

Simplifying Complicated Ideas

Complex concepts are frequently intricate thought processes that are capable of being deconstructed into simpler and more fundamental ideas. Mind maps visually break down a large, central concept into smaller, more easily comprehensible bits of information. They can store and structure large amounts of information within a relatively compact and well-appointed space.

Mind mapping's simplifying capability is particularly powerful when used in group work. Collaboration among team members is vastly improved when they work with visual tools, familiar data structures, and commonly understood keywords.

Enhancing Creativity

Mind mapping is designed to "entice, delight, stimulate, and challenge" us. [9] Persons making their own mind maps of the same topic seldom end up with exactly the same mind map. Chances are, they would be markedly different because mind maps are often unique, personalized pictures of their creators' perceptions. When we create maps, our basic instincts tell us to make them appealing, attractive, and understandable to ourselves, even if we do not consciously try to do so. Our respective viewpoints will guide the way we organize the topics in relative proximity to each other.

Constructing effective mind maps uses graphic devices such as lines, symbols, colors, and images together with words to create a multi-dimensional learning and memory tool. But we apply these elements to the degree that we are comfortable with them. Artistic people will likely make a masterpiece of their mind maps. Those who prefer simple, unadorned keywords will probably stick to creating labeled branches and little else. Most of us will create mind maps that are somewhere in between the two extremes.

Quicker Note-Taking And Review

All of us have taken notes, not only while studying but even at work. We also take informal notes at random times, such as when we want to keep a recipe or remember a friend's number. Note-taking is our go-to method when we want to recall something later. Aside from referral and remembering, we also take notes to enhance our concentration, to understand something, and to revise what we already remember. [10]

During those instances, we need to take notes in real-time, such as when we try to capture a lecture while it is delivered. Our first impulse is to attempt to jot down every word the lecturer says. Failing that, we take down phrases and snatches of an idea, thinking to later rewrite them in an outline or other form. While performing the note-taking shortcuts, we frequently draw lines, shapes, or arrows between the concepts to help us remember special relationships that link them. A great alternative is to draw a mind map (or something close to it) that approximates these shortcuts and allows us to keep pace with the lecture.

Employing Spatial Mnemonics

Mnemonics is a word we often hear but are seldom familiar with. It is defined as the development of systems for improving the memory. Frequently, we associate it with assembling the initials of a set of words we wish to remember and creating a sentence or phrase out of it. In music, the notes on the lines of the G-clef are best remembered by the sentence, "Every Good Boy Does Fine," while the notes on the spaces spell out the word "FACE." Here, the sentence and the word are known as mnemonic devices.

Mnemonic Devices To Remember Musical Notes

Every Good Boy Does Fine   FACE

Spatial mnemonics is a memory system grounded in the location of things. You may have known some eccentric people whose study would be strewn with books, papers, and whatnot, yet would strongly warn anybody against tidying up the place because "there is an order to this chaos." That is because they remember where things were placed amid the clutter, such that relocating the things in the course of cleaning would, in their minds, place their personal effects in disarray.

The theory of spatial mnemonics in mind maps is that lists of words can also be remembered better if they are arranged in a distinctive pattern. The mind map provides that pattern, such that if we wish to remember the information under the topics and subtopics, we could try to recall their location in the mind map and the keywords with which they are adjacent. At least one academic research found that medical students learned their lessons and recalled what they had studied more easily using mind mapping techniques. [11] Since the field of medicine, like most scientific disciplines, requires much memory work, medical students will greatly benefit from applying mind mapping to their lessons.

Mind maps have many advantages, but they also have their disadvantages, some of which are:

- *Lack of standards*
- *May be inadequate in explaining highly complex concepts*
- *May be unsuitable for some interlinked associations*
- *Can be easy to overcomplicate*
- *Limited extensibility*

Let us examine these disadvantages and see how we can overcome them.

Lack Of Standards

While mind maps have gained wide acceptance and popularity, their construction remains highly variable and unstandardized. Mind maps are, after all, representations of information as they are understood by the map's creator. There is no set of rules or conventions that is universally followed in the creation and interpretation of mind maps. This makes the accurate interpretation of a particular mind map known only to its maker or the relative few who may have collaborated to make it, such as in the case of a team brainstorming session. The lack of a standard makes mind mapping a personal (or limited) tool for accurately conveying information.

While the lack of standards may create some difficulty in interpreting others' mind maps, this may be overcome by notations during the documentation of the map. Documentation is also useful for the creator's own purposes so that revisiting the mind map in the future would make recalling the details of its construction easier.

May Be Inadequate In Explaining Highly Complex Concepts

At its best, a mind map is an intuitive device. It draws connections between related ideas, but it cannot explain the nature of their relationships except as the keywords linking them may suggest. Complex concepts may at times be broken down into simpler ideas – this is the premise behind the simplifying capability of mind maps. But some concepts require explicit definition, description, and thorough explanation to be fully comprehended and appreciated.

Take the situation where specialists in various fields of expertise perform the difficult task of transmitting their vast knowledge gained through years of study and experience to their young proteges. These proteges, in turn, would someday also teach the next generation what they have been taught, as well as what they have learned from experience. Knowledge of medicine, for instance, has been handed down from the time of Hippocrates in ancient Greece some 2,400 years ago to physicians today. For complex ideas in expert fields to survive the millennia, they must be accurately and thoroughly explained to preserve them for the whole of civilization. The teaching of complex concepts may be aided by a mind map, but cannot be replaced by it.

To overcome this difficulty, attach your source notes or outlines to the finished mind map. Information changes over time, and the source notes would be indispensable to fill in the gaps that mind maps will necessarily have when selecting topics and keywords to include in the diagram, even for relatively uncomplicated material. We should not forget that the mind map is a memory tool situated in a particular time and place. Its truncated nature may leave out details we may need in the future.

May Be Unsuitable For Some Interlinked Associations

In general, mind maps are circular, nonlinear tools for organizing information. Therefore, if a theme or topic consists of purely linear associations, then the "mind map" reduces to a mere linear diagram. As you will see in

Chapter 7, which discusses the different types of mind maps, there is a flow map that is linear in form. It is still a mind map, but it does not have the radially-emanating multiple branches.

The situation where a mind map may not be applicable has to do with interlinked concepts that have multiple relationships between them. For mind maps to work, the associations between concepts should not be interlinked; rather, the topics should have a simple one-to-one relationship. [12] Interlinked concepts are best represented in a concept map, such as the one shown below.

Interlinked Relationships In A Concept Map [13]

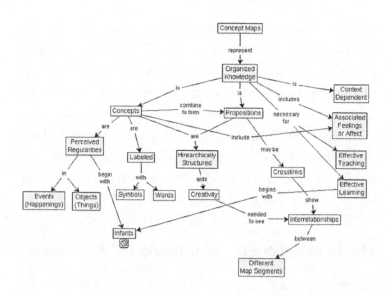

Notice how the connectors can branch out from and combine with one or more concepts. The structure significantly differs from the contemporary mind maps shown in the preceding chapters, where smaller branches are linked to a single, larger branch, and the largest branches connect directly to the central concept.

In a subsequent chapter, we will be introduced to types of mind maps, known as system maps, that allow for some level of interconnection similar to concept maps. This is enabled by a higher level of sophistication provided by digital mind mapping tools available online. Generally, however, manually created mind maps are not suited to interlinked associations such as those in concept maps.

Concept maps and mind maps are similar in so far as they both rely on the constructivist approach in the learning-teaching process. Constructivism holds that learners actively construct or create knowledge rather than just passively take in information. [14] We experience the world and reflect upon those experiences. Our minds then build unique representations of these reflections and assimilate the new information into our pre-existing mental models (or schemas) stored in long-term memory. The schemas comprise the structures by which we organize information about the world.

Can Be Easy To Overcomplicate

Sometimes, when a topic is unusually broad and complex, we get carried away when creating a mind map that tries to include all the topics that we feel are important. The branches run off into many sub-branches and twigs, cluttering the visuals and making the entire map challenging to comprehend fully. There are methods by which we can simplify the mind map's presentation without sacrificing all the important details we want to include.

If you are plotting your mind map on paper, you can create sub-maps for branches that lead to many important sub-topics. On the main map, construct the branch labeled with its keyword, attaching a connector (for instance, an arrow or circle with the notation "Sub-map A") to indicate that details of the branch are continued on another page. Then on the duly marked "Sub-map A," draw the branch keyword as the central theme and proceed, as you would, to elaborate on its details. You can have as many sub-maps as you need. They provide the advantage of focusing attention on this important topic without detracting from its relationship with the central concept on the main map.

Mind mapping software has powerful tools that can help you simplify your mind map. Chapter 9 presents these in greater detail with its discussion of commercially available mind mapping applications. [15]

Limited Extensibility

Alsuraihi [16] identified a few drawbacks of mind mapping, one of which is limited extensibility – the degree to which mind maps may be expanded or stretched. Hand-drawn mind maps understandably have a limitation of physical space, if one of the requisites was for the map to occupy a single page. The dimensions of the page would be the limit of the map's extensibility.

Even with hand-drawn maps, however, limited extensibility may be overcome with some creativity. Using the same methods as those to address overcomplication, we could construct sub-maps on other pages and link them to the main map by attaching connectors to one of the man map's branches. The case is different with digital mind maps. Virtual mind maps are infinitely expandable because space is unlimited. This is further explained in Chapter 9.

Action Steps

Mind mapping has both advantages and disadvantages. Whether one outweighs the other depends on two things: the user (or users) and the information being mapped. Keep this in mind when answering the following questions:

1. When can mind maps improve communications between different people, and when can they not help people communicate better?

2. When can mind maps simplify concepts, and when can they complicate them even more?

3. When can mind maps be easy to create and organize ideas with, and when can they be more difficult?

After you mull these questions over, turn over to the end of this chapter and see if you concur with the answers given.

Moving On

Like any tool or device, mind mapping helps some people more than others. Its potential to benefit you can only be explored if you use it to accomplish tasks that are important to you. If you have not tried it yet, turn the page to the next chapter and learn how to make your first mind map.

Key Takeaways

1. Mind maps have many forms but all possess five characteristics. They have a main subject conspicuously located in the diagram. Major themes radiate as branches from the main subject. Each branch is identified by a keyword or idea. Less important topics emanate as twigs from the branches. Finally, topics located closer to the main theme are more important, while those located farther away are less important.

2. The advantageous characteristics of mind mapping include:

- *Compatible with the brain*
- *Provides balance with the brain*
- *Use keywords*
- *Simplify complicated examples*

- *Enhance creativity*
- *Quick note-taking and review*
- *Employ special mnemonics*

3. The disadvantageous traits of mind mapping include:

- *Lack of standards*
- *Inadequate for intricate explanations*
- *Unsuitable for interlinked associations*
- *Can be easy to overcomplicate*
- *Limited extensibility*

Answers to the action steps:

1. Mind maps improve communications between users who share a common background and knowledge concerning the mapped information. A mind map that was drawn intuitively in a manner that is meaningful personally to the creator may not effectively convey the same meaning to other users.

2. Mind maps can simplify concepts that are sufficiently limited in scope to be contained in a physical diagram. They can complicate the information even more if the information has a scope too broad to be accommodated in a physically-drawn diagram. A complicated body of information must be broken down into manageable parts for diagramming. Also, no matter how well a mind map is constructed, it can never fully substitute for original information not commonly known.

3. The ease with which mind maps can be created depends on the skill of the user and the medium used. Long-time mind mappers know how to break down and efficiently organize information reflected in the mind map, while novices will struggle with what to include and how to represent them. Also, hand-drawn mind maps will require repeatedly revising with an eraser and pencil before the creator is satisfied and redraws the final mind map with ink. Digital mind maps allow for instantaneous changes and limitless opportunities for revisions over time.

5

MIND MAP MASTERY

CONQUER MIND MAPS AND CREATE YOURS USING THIS EASY-TO-USE STEP-BY-STEP PROCESS

W ho are familiar with a social media platform called Facebook? Let's rephrase the question: who is not familiar with Facebook? It is almost a sure bet that there are fewer people in modern societies who do not have a Facebook profile than those who do. Launched in 2004, it provided a wonderful way for people to keep in touch with family and friends while making new acquaintances.

In contrast to Facebook's wide popularity, its predecessor, a Seattle-based social networking service called Classmates.com, is known only by a relative few. Classmates.com was launched in 1995 by former Boeing manager Randy Conrads. [1] As its name suggests, the service helped users find classmates and colleagues from kindergarten to college, and even at workplaces and the U.S. military. Users create a basic profile providing their name, graduation date, birthday, and email address. They subsequently build on the profile by uploading a profile photo and other information about themselves. The site's search engine then allows users to view other people who went to the same school they attended and the year they graduated. This fulfills the main goal of the site: to enable users to locate and keep in touch with their former classmates.

Conceptualizing a social networking site like Classmates.com is instinctual. Specifying a few search criteria increases the probability of finding the right connections: school, location, year, program, degree, and other qualifiers in users' profiles. Conceptually, the search branches out from general to specific criteria, connecting people with the same profile characteristics.

Classmates.com is a digital network that works by clustering people. In this sense, it is similar to a mind map which is a visual network that "clusters ideas." It is a way of collecting and grouping certain ideas focused on a specific topic and defined by correlated connections. [2] A network of connections will necessarily have things that are connected – people in social networks, and topics in a mind mapping network. It will also have the connecting pathways, the nodes that locate the connections, and the structure that informatively organizes the elements.

Elements Of A Mind Map

A social networking site is difficult to create. A mind map is a great deal easier to make. It requires a few fundamental components that are standard for all mind maps. They are used to organize a cluster of random yet specific ideas that, in the end, will take the form of an organized network.

1. Central theme/idea

The main topic for which the mind map is constructed is known as the central theme or idea. It is the most important topic and is the concept with the broadest scope in the mind map. The central theme is essential in any mind map; without it, no mind map can be drawn.

2. Subtopics or keywords

The subtopics are the next-level components after the central theme. They refer to the details of the central theme. Each subtopic is information about the main idea that is encapsulated in a single keyword (or phrase at most). The keyword summarizes the information which otherwise would have been expressed in sentences; therefore, the choice of the keyword is important as it should represent the essence of the information.

3. Associations (Branches and sub-branches)

Associations are collectively the extension of the central idea. The subtopics and keywords comprise the associations. Subtopics and keywords linked directly to the main theme are known as first-level associations. Subtopics and keywords linked to the first-level associations are second-level associations, and so forth. A mind map may theoretically have an unlimited number of first-level associations, but the mind can grasp a maximum of about seven first-level associations. This is not a hard-and-fast rule, but limiting each level to seven associations aids in improving recall of the mind map.

4. Relationship connections

Relationship connections link the main idea to topics, which in turn are similarly linked to their sub-topics, and so on. The connectors may be lines or arrows that radiate from the center or emanate from higher-level associations. The lines or arrows are the visual representation of the branches and twigs in the network. Curved lines are advisable because our brain can more easily distinguish them in the illustration.

5. Proximity

Proximity refers to the physical distance of related keywords. When creating a mind map, it is important to keep associated keywords in closer proximity to each other. Lines linking ideas that situate them farther apart suggest to the viewer that the ideas are less closely related, or possibly unrelated. Keywords viewed in closer proximity are more easily memorized and recalled in conjunction with each other.

6. Colors, images, and shapes

A mind map can be a more effective memory or learning tool if it is enhanced by such components are colors, images, and shapes. These elements improve the visibility of the mind map particularly for visual learners, who comprise about 65 percent of the general population. [3]

Visual elements make mind maps more easily readable and understandable for the vast majority of learners and mind map users.

Steps In Creating A Mind Map

There are only four simple steps in creating a mind map.

<u>Step 1:</u> Start by drawing a central concept. If you are creating your mind map by hand drawing it on paper, locate the central idea in the center of the page.

<u>Step 2:</u> Develop the main ideas relating to this central concept. For each of the main ideas, construct a line connecting it to the main concept. Consider these as branches, and be sure to label them with keywords, one keyword per branch.

<u>Step 3:</u> Generate sub-branches, or "twigs," out of each branch, representing related ideas and topics. These sub-branches may be developed further into smaller twigs representing ideas with narrower scope but increasing detail. As in the preceding step, label each sub-branch with its corresponding keyword.

<u>Step 4:</u> Apply different colors, symbols, and images to visually differentiate among the topics and sub-topics.

Those are the four steps to creating a mind map. They appear deceptively simple, but the difficulty of their execution depends on the complexity of the main topic and the mind map creator's skill in organizing the topics or ideas. The map's artistry relies not only on the ability but also the need of the creator for imagery. Thus, step 4 is important only to the degree that the map's user deems visual enhancements to be necessary. While many mind mapping instructional websites may urge to maximize the use of colors and images, this is not always advisable. Some users may find multiple visual elements distracting, thus enhancements should be applied judiciously and only when users find them truly helpful.

A Quick Example

Let us plan something that requires some complexity – say, a traditional Latin American church wedding. This is usually a year-long (or even longer) undertaking, and no matter how much time the happy couple takes, there are always last-minute issues. So, a mind map is a useful tool to prepare beforehand, as it is open to limitless and frequent modifications until the happy day itself.

We start the mind map with the central theme.

Wedding Plan Mind Map 1

Wedding Plan

With this in mind, we start brainstorming random ideas that are necessary for a traditional church wedding. Intuitively, we know that the church must be decided upon, so we list this. Then the bride and groom name the special people they usually kept closest in mind for the occasion, maybe for years – the maid of honor and the best man. Other people they need to decide on are the principal and secondary sponsors, the bridesmaids and ushers, and the adorable children in the entourage – the ring and coin bearers and the flower girls. Then the bride, groom, and entourage should necessarily be dressed, so clothing should be listed. And, of course, they should choose their rings. Other lesser but necessary items in a traditional wedding include the reception, arrhae, veil, cord, flowers, invitations, and so on.

These are all related to the wedding, so we reason, let's put them all in the mind map. The result will be like this:

Wedding Plan Mind Map 2

Immediately, we see that this will not work as a planning tool because the mind map is too cumbersome and inefficient for either planning or remembering. Besides, we should keep in mind the rule of thumb that the mind can remember best up to seven items. So, let us group some items.

There are several people in our list above whom we can collectively call the "Entourage." Other items, such as the cord, veil, rings, etc., are needed for the church ceremony, so let us group them under "Church." With these two steps alone, we reduce our mind map to the following:

Wedding Plan Mind Map 3

Now let's add the other items under their proper categories, and some other items as well.

Wedding Plan Mind Map 4

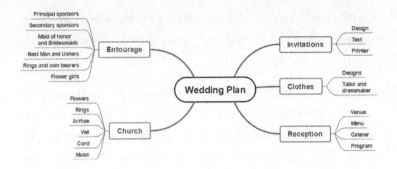

Wedding Mind Map 4 is a great improvement over Wedding Mind Map 2 (the first attempt to expand the main theme) because it has limited first-level associations, enhancing its memorability. Wedding Mind Map 4 is also an improvement over Mind Map 3 because it incorporates the other items earlier identified during brainstorming and makes the proper connections to the first-level concepts with which they are related. While Wedding Mind Map 4 is already a useful diagram for planning, it may still be improved in case further items need to be included. Artistic devices such as colors, shapes, and images may be added if they are helpful to the users, so their usefulness must be weighed against the amount of clutter they may likely introduce to the mind map.

<u>An Alternative Way</u>

In the Wedding Plan Mind Map example, we went about creating the mind map using an intuitive pathway – that is, we brainstormed related items before categorizing those closely connected to reduce the number of first-level associations. We then built the second-level associations out of those items that were grouped together. We used nothing more than intuition and common sense in gathering related items.

Sometimes, there are types of information that come to us in a pre-structured format. Outlines of lessons are one of them. Supposing you were studying the history of Japan. In your research, you came across its timeline but still found it hard to memorize. It appears in table form on the next page. The table was prepared by Dr. Amy Vladeck Heinrich of Columbia University as a guide for students of Asian history. It is a comprehensive collection of information that many students may not find easy to commit to memory.

Timeline Of Japanese History [4]

Early Period	
ca 4000 BCE	**Jomon**
	Prehistoric culture characterized by handmade pottery with rope pattern design
Ca 300 BCE	**Yayoi Culture**
	More advanced agricultural society, using metals and wheel-turned pottery
ca 300 CE	**Tomb Period**
	KOFUN (250-538) | ASUKA (538-710)
	Great earthen grave mounds and their funerary objects, such as clay haniwa — terra cotta figurines of people and animals, models of buildings and boats — attest to emergence of powerful clan rulers. Among these was the Yamato clan, whose rulers began the imperial dynasty that has continued to the present.
Classical Period	
552 CE	Introduction of Buddhism
645 CE	**Taika Reform**
	Reorganization and reform based largely on learning imported from China: Buddhism, writing system, bureaucratic organization, legal theories
710-814 CE	**Nara Period**
	Establishment of first permanent capital at Nara; emergence of Japanese patterns of administration and institutions. Beginning of classical period.
794-1185 CE	Heian Period; Late Heian (Fujiwara)
	Great flowering of classical Japanese culture in new capital of Heian-kyo (Kyoto). Court aristocracy, especially women, produced great body of literature — poetry, diaries, the novel The Tale of Genji — and made refined aesthetic sensibility their society's hallmark.
Medieval Period	
1185-1333 CE	**Kamakura Period**
	Beginning of military rule, as samurai (warriors) replaced nobles as real rulers of Japan. Imperial court remained in Kyoto but shoguns governing organization based in Kamakura, south of modern Tokyo.
1333-1336 CE	Kemmu Restoration
1336-1573 CE	**Ashikaga (Muromachi) Period**
	New warrior government in Kyoto retained weak control of the country, but from its base in Kyoto's Muromachi district became patron of newly flourishing artistic tradition, influenced by Zen Buddhist culture as well as samurai and court society.
	Country at War
	Warring factions engaged in lengthy, destructive civil wars
1568-1598 CE	Unification
1600-1867 CE	**Tokugawa (Edo) Period**
	Country unified under military government which maintained 250 years of secluded peace, leading to development of vibrant urban, "middle-class" culture with innovations in economic organization, literature, and the arts.
Modern Period	
1868-1912 CE	Meiji Restoration
	MEIJI ERA
	Emergence, with Western stimulus, into modern international world, marked by dramatic alterations in institutions, traditional social organization, and culture.
1912-1926 CE	Taisho Era
1926-1989 CE	Showa Era
1945-present*	Contemporary Japan:
	HEISEI ERA (1989-PRESENT)
	REIWA (2019-PRESENT)

A mind map may be helpful here. We start with the main theme.

Japanese History Mind Map 1

To this central theme, we attach connectors to the first-level connections. The spider chart form is useful in identifying the hierarchy of topics, the topmost layer of which consists of the historical periods.

Our mind map can be expanded like this:

Japanese History Mind Map 2

The number of first-level associations is well below the seven associations in our rule-of-thumb, therefore, we shall let it stand. We then proceed to the information in the first two columns of the chart. Immediately, we have the sub-periods and their time durations. These could well comprise the second-level (and some third-level) associations, further expanding our mind map as follows:

Japanese History Mind Map 3

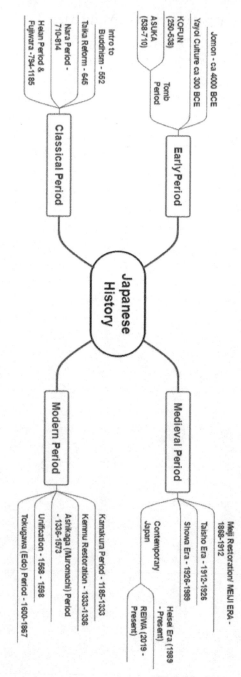

Japanese History

Early Period
- Jomon - ca 4000 BCE
- Yayoi Culture ca 300 BCE
- KOFUN (250-538) — Tomb Period
- ASUKA (538-710) — Tomb Period
- Intro to Buddhism - 552

Classical Period
- Taika Reform - 645
- Nara Period - 710-814
- Heian Period & Fujiwara - 794-1185

Medieval Period
- Meiji Restoration/ MEIJI ERA - 1868-1912
- Taisho Era - 1912-1926
- Showa Era - 1926-1989
- Contemporary Japan — Heisei Era (1989 - Present)
- Contemporary Japan — REIWA (2019 - Present)

Modern Period
- Kamakura Period - 1185-1333
- Kenmu Restoration - 1333-1336
- Ashikaga (Muromachi) Period - 1336-1573
- Unification - 1568 - 1598
- Tokugawa (Edo) Period - 1600-1867

At this point, we notice that our mind map has reached a level of complexity that is beginning to challenge our ability to comprehend at one glance. Nevertheless, the visual placement of the first, second, and, in two instances, third-level associations gives us a picture that aids in memorizing which particular period the sub-periods are associated with. The advantage of the mind map over the chart is its potential for spatial mnemonics. Recall this concept in the preceding chapter. The arrangement of the sub-periods in a distinctive pattern and location in the mind map, as well as their proximity to their respective periods, helps their easier recall. It is similar to the memory palace where their location serves as a memory aid.

Also, note our inability to add further levels onto the mind map. This demonstrates the limited extensibility of a two-dimensional mind map, also discussed in Chapter 4. Although there remains much more information in the chart, further extending the mind map above makes it complicated, defeating the mind map's purpose of simplifying. However, as we explained in that chapter, the way to overcome this limitation is by attaching sub-mind maps by taking a subtopic and making this a main topic in an attached mind map. This may be done in hand-drawn mind maps but is better undertaken by using mind map software programs.

Action Steps

Two mind map illustrations were shown in this chapter. One is the wedding plan mind map and the other is the Japanese history mind map. Their results are Wedding Plan Mind Map 4 and Japan History Mind Map 3, respectively. Let us presume that you did not know how each was developed and you were only presented with the two results.

1. Will you be confident that you understand Wedding Plan Mind Map 4 sufficiently to explain it in your own words?
2. Could you say the same about Japan History Mind Map 3?
3. Recall how the answers at the end of Chapter 4 anchor the benefits of mind map on users' backgrounds and the nature of the topic. How would you explain the difference in the ease of interpretation between the two mind map results?

Moving On

The steps in creating a mind map can be deceptively easy because as the Japanese History Mind Map exercise shows, not all information can be contained in the final diagram. As the action step exercise shows, the purpose of the mind determines the adequacy of the result. In the next chapter, we look at the different uses of the mind map.

Key Takeaways

1. The elements of a mind map include the central theme or idea, subtopics or keywords, associations or branches, relationship connections, proximity, and colors, images and shapes.

2. There are four steps to create a mind map:

- *Draw a central concept.*
- *Develop main ideas relating to the central concept.*
- *Generate more details for the main ideas.*
- *Apply visual effects to enhance the map.*

3. Mind maps may be created intuitively, but they may also be developed from intermediate tools such as outlines and tables that organize the ideas.

6

PUTTING MIND MAPS IN ACTION

USING MIND MAPS IN YOUR DAILY LIVES AND GET TANGIBLE AND AUTHENTIC RESULTS

" A good tool improves the way you work. A great tool improves the way you think." - Jeff Duntemann, author and editor, software technologies [1]

Tools are devices, real or virtual, that help us carry out certain functions. Carpentry tools are examples of real tools with which we do woodwork. Using conventional tools such as handheld hammers and saws helps a skilled carpenter create good furniture. A carpenter who works with power hammers and saws would likely create furniture just as well, even if he were not as skilled. Power tools are good tools because they improve the way we work.

On the other hand, wood carving tools in the hands of an artist help him fashion the images he envisions in his mind. Chisels, gouges, veins, and other specialized tools free a woodcarver to create exquisite artwork that amazes, delights, and inspires.

Thai-Style Wood Carving [2]

Simply stated, some tools help us perform the basics, while other tools enable us to transcend the common and mundane.

What is true of physical tools is also true of mental tools - we use them to achieve the purposes for which we aim, whether fundamental or sublime. Mind mapping is a mental tool. It helps us perform basic, everyday activities such as note-taking, learning, and memorizing. But it also enables us to perform higher-level mental processes such as analyzing, organizing, and creating. The preceding chapter introduced us to the components of mind mapping and some fundamental techniques for creating mind maps. The simple examples and observations we arrived at about them must have provided us insights into their many possible uses.

Let us briefly revisit three basic functions mind mapping supports.

1. Quicker note-taking

The typical note-taking methods include writing in shorthand, outlining, or transcribing texts verbatim. Shorthand note-taking requires specialized training discontinued from current curricula, while outlining and transcribing are wieldy and cause students to lag behind the lecturer and miss important notes. Those who master the skill of mind mapping are capable of taking notes more completely and quickly because they reduce the words they write with keywords or short phrases connected by lines, shapes, and other visual devices. Mind mapping allows note-takers to keep pace with the train of thought pursued in lectures and presentations.

2. Improved learning

When learners create mind maps, they are actively engaged in digesting and analyzing the material they are studying. Their engagement goes deeper than merely memorizing words which many students equate to learning. Identifying keywords requires the mind to understand the discussion sufficiently to encapsulate it. Drawing lines creates associations that organize and structure the lesson. Incorporating artistic devices captures the learner's interest and excitement during the "aha!" moment – the moment of insight into a new idea.

3. Better memory retention

Creating mind maps activates many levels of brain activity, engaging both the left and right lobes. When more areas of the brain are engaged in "digesting" a concept, the mind will be better at ingraining, retaining, and recalling the concept from memory when needed. This makes mind maps a great memory tool not only for lessons but for any sort of information worth committing to memory.

Mind maps enhance many basic functions, but their full power extends to many uses beyond the fundamentals. To fully appreciate the versatility of this mental tool, let us see some examples of mind mapping that served specific purposes.

Studying

Earlier, we mentioned that mind mapping improves learning. As a general undertaking, learning covers many different situations, such as learning a hobby, a skill, or a life lesson. Studying is a type of learning whereby a student devotes serious time, attention, and sustained effort to acquire knowledge, particularly from books, in an academic setting.

Mind maps are particularly useful in organizing knowledge that covers a broad area. In our civics classes, we learned about the government, how it is structured, and how it works. The following is a mind map of this lesson.

U.S. Government Mind Map

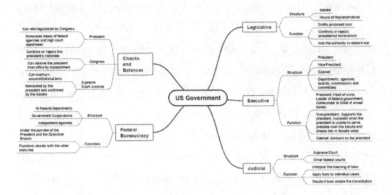

US Government

Legislative
- Structure
  - Senate
  - House of Representatives
- Function
  - Drafts proposed laws
  - Confirms or rejects presidential nominations
  - Has the authority to declare war

Executive
- Structure
  - President
  - Vice-President
  - Cabinet
  - Departments, agencies, boards, commissions and committees
- Function
  - President: Head of state, Leader of federal government, Commander in Chief of armed forces
  - Vice-president: Supports the president, succeeds when the president is unable to serve, presides over the Senate and breaks ties in Senate votes
  - Cabinet: Advisors to the president

Judicial
- Structure
  - Supreme Court
  - Other federal courts
- Function
  - Interpret the meaning of laws
  - Apply laws to individual cases
  - Decide if laws violate the Constitution

Checks and Balances
- President
  - Can veto legislation by Congress
  - Nominates heads of federal agencies and high court appointees
- Congress
  - Confirms or rejects the president's nominees
  - Can remove the president from office by impeachment
- Supreme Court Justices
  - Can overturn unconstitutional laws
  - Nominated by the president and confirmed by the Senate

Federal Bureaucracy
- Structure
  - 15 Federal Departments
  - Government Corporations
  - Independent Agencies
- Functions
  - Under the purview of the President and the Executive Branch
  - Functions closely with the other branches

The main theme of the mind map is about the government, in this case, the U.S. Government, so this goes to the center of the mind map. There are five main sub-topics: the three branches of government (Legislative, Executive, and Judicial), the Federal Bureaucracy, which is the machinery that supports the three branches, and Checks and Balances which is the rationale behind the government's structure and function. This mind map could be further expanded with the use of a digital mind map platform, but by itself, the diagram is a well-organized, capsule-size introductory course to the U.S. government. After a deep reading of the chapter, this mind map will be a good way to review and remember the lesson.

Writing

Mind mapping is a visual tool that helps us organize and structure information. It is therefore a great aid when we organize our thoughts before putting them into writing. Essays, novels, reports, and other written work deliver an author's message more effectively if they are organized well. The ideal form and substance of a literary piece depend on its genre, so for our example, we shall mind map how a novel is plotted before being written out.

Plotting A Novel Mind Map

The mind map shown above is a generic example for plotting a novel. The key themes that must be addressed include the characters, the status quo or opening situation, the motivation behind each character, the initiating incident, the development, the crisis or climax, and the resolution or denouement. As we plot the novel, we fill in the details, changing ideas as we finalize the plot. Then as parts of the novel are written, we can use the mind map as our guide so that the narrative we are building does not stray too far from the plot's design.

Mind maps of narratives may be similar to each other because they have the same elements. Novels are, however, many times more complex than short stories or simpler narratives. We can, therefore, expect the full-blown version of the novel-plotting mind map to be expanded to many sub-mind maps, each focusing on a specific element of the main mind map. Other literary genres, such as essays and reports, will have different sets of topics altogether. But they all serve the same purpose – to aid the writer in planning out the piece to be written and to guide him or her as the writing progresses.

Brainstorming

Brainstorming is a method by which a group of people rapidly generate ideas for planning or solving problems. Sometimes brainstorming may be performed by a single person, but it finds its greatest benefit when performed by several people. Group brainstorming also faces a greater challenge in bringing together the thoughts and ideas of people who think differently to arrive at a consensus agreed to by all.

Let us suppose that a group is tasked to make plans for a school's foundation day. It is an important celebration, so the administration decided that the different members of the school community should provide their input. Four groups are represented in the planning committee: the students, their parents, the school faculty, and the school employees. The mind map below is an example of the results of the first planning session.

Brainstorming Mind Map

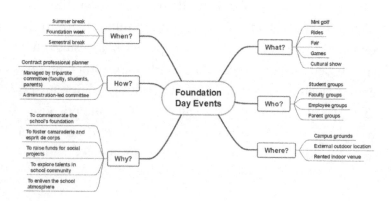

To arrive at this mind map, representatives of the four groups got together in the brainstorming session. The aim was to make tentative suggestions but not yet formulate a final decision. Since this is an event, the options to six basic questions comprised the first-level association – the what, who, where, when, how, and why of the foundation day activities. The answers to the questions formed enumerations of responses that constitute the second-level associations. For this brainstorming mind map, there is no need to extend beyond the second-level associations because brainstorming precludes any analysis or details about the suggested ideas.

A mind map helps bring a group of people to a common understanding because it is simple and visual. People speaking with each other often fail to grasp what everyone says during the conversation because they may be lost in their own thoughts or may fail to comprehend what the others are saying. Spoken words are ephemeral and are immediately lost the moment they are articulated. Merely listing suggestions helps the group focus better. However, drawing a mind map during brainstorming captures the session as it progresses and creates a visual record understood by all the participants. This makes mind mapping a particularly useful brainstorming tool.

Decision-Making

Nearly everyone knows instinctively what decision-making is because we have instinctively made decisions since as far back as we can remember. A decision is a choice made among two or more options. The steps in a decision-making process may be simple or complex, depending upon the difficulty of the goal to be achieved and the consequences of failure to attain the goal.

The following mind map is a template that would prove useful for making mostly personal decisions. It is quite simple, beginning with some basic background knowledge against which a goal is set. The goal is frequently vague and abstract, such as achieving personal success; thus, it needs to be broken down into smaller, actionable objectives.

Decision-Making Mind Map

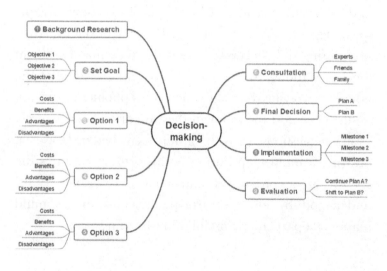

Out of the objectives set, alternative actions are formulated to attain them. Considerations based on their costs, benefits, advantages, and disadvantages become the bases of the choice to be made. Validation of the possible choice is performed by consulting friends, family, and experts (as well as reference groups such as social media circles). The final decision (Plan A) may leave room for change (Plan B) if, after implementation, the desired goal is not met.

Many would equate decision-making with problem-solving because there are so many parallels between them. It would be more accurate, however, to think of decision-making as the final step in solving a problem.

Problem-Solving

The next mind map illustrates the problem-solving process for academic studies such as theses and dissertations, although it may be adopted in solving most problems that require the rigorous analysis of standardized data. The latter would include problems with applications in business (financial, operational, or marketing problems), economics, public governance, and other fields.

The first problem-solving mind map on the next page is in the typical spider web form. The second mind map is the same as the first, except that it is rendered in tree form, which enhances the readability of the labels in the branches and twigs. The numbered topics branching out from the central theme suggest the sequence according to which each topic is undertaken in the problem-solving process. The choice of form depends on the preference of the user.

Problem-Solving Mind Map, Spider Diagram

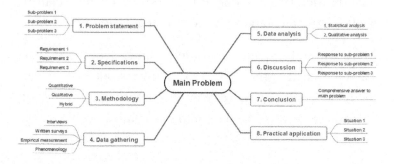

Problem-Solving Mind Map, Tree Diagram

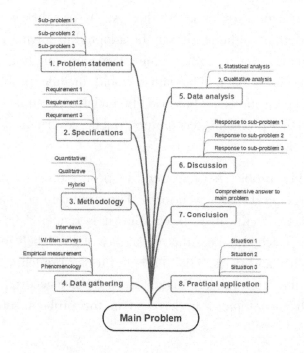

Project Management

A project is an activity or undertaking that has a definite beginning and end. It is usually broad in scope and complex in execution, such that it needs to be carefully planned. Not all planned activities are projects – for instance, an ongoing business is not a project because it is not intended to end at a definite time. Projects have a specific goal, and when that goal has been attained, the project is terminated.

The project involves numerous elements that may be easily overlooked if they are not managed systematically. The following mind map provides a comprehensive overview of a project plan's important aspects and will make a great tool for a manager to keep track of the project's advancement.

Project Management Mind Map

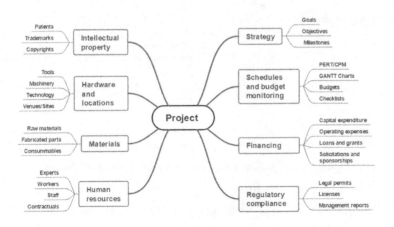

Mind maps can supplement project plans; they cannot, however, replace them. Mind maps provide the overview but will require almost unlimited extensibility to contain all the necessary details of a project plan. On the other hand, all kinds of plans can be aided by mind maps, as the next section explains.

Planning

A plan is a proposal or intention to do something. Going by this definition, practically all the foregoing mind maps in this chapter are plans of some sort. Mind maps can be used to create generic plans, such as the wedding plan mind map presented in <u>Chapter 5</u> and reproduced below.

Wedding Plan Mind Map

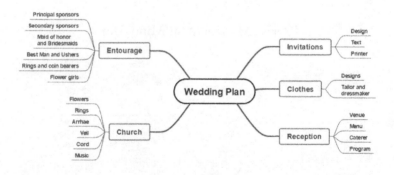

Planning for an event is always a work in progress until the event is held. So, too, is the mind map for the event. The deceptively simplistic initial mind map may grow in complexity as new ideas are conceived, and fresh details are added. Changes are also to be expected, so consider saving the evolving versions of the mind map in case you would want to reconsider the revisions made.

Presentation

Mind maps can be used for presentations. A simple "static" mind map can be a good visual aid, but even better would be a mind map that works as a dynamic slideshow, wherein clicking on the topics opens up slides that depict and explain what the particular topic is about. Mind map software with slideshow features or templates is available online.

Let us use the Wedding Plan mind map shown in the preceding section of this chapter. If this were made into a slideshow presentation, clicking on "Designs" related to "Clothes" would open a series of photos showing the gowns of the bride, groom, and entourage. The mind map app may zoom in closer to that subtopic to magnify the slide show. Clicking to leave the topic will close the slide show and zoom out to, once again, show the full view of the main mind map.

Below is an illustration of how clicking on a topic of the digital mind map presentation enlarges that branch and opens a slide show of that topic.

Wedding Plan Mind Map Presentation

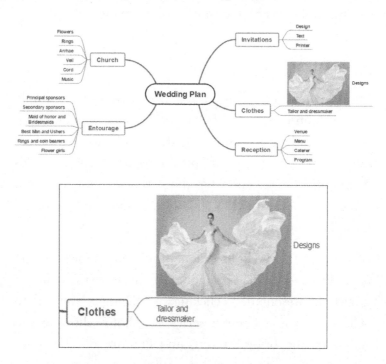

In Chapter 9 of this book, we will review some of the digital mind mapping tools currently available and what advanced features they have over manual mind mapping. For now, what is useful to remember is that the ability to create animated and slide show presentations is available to enhance the extensibility and complexity beyond that of a two-dimensional mind map.

Action Steps

This chapter describes three general functions and eight specific uses of mind maps. For sure, not all of us will be needing mind maps for all these purposes, since not all of them are relevant to us individually.

For this exercise, choose from among the five topics suggested below. Your choice will likely be aligned with your needs so you should have some background knowledge about it. (Better yet, if you have a topic you would want to work on, feel free to use that.) Create a mind map on your selected topic, aiming for a result that will be truly useful to you.

1. Plan for your next out-of-town vacation.
2. Describe how to prepare your next income tax return.
3. Prepare to host the next family Thanksgiving dinner.
4. Present a sales pitch for your company's new product launch.
5. Outline how to decide on your next job to move up your career ladder.

Moving On

Mind mapping has the versatility and flexibility to be used to achieve numerous goals. To attain various purposes, mind maps can assume different forms. The next chapter will introduce us to some of these mind map forms beyond the basic spider diagram.

Key Takeaways

1. Traditionally, the three basic uses of mind maps are for quicker note-taking, improved learning, and better memory retention.
2. Some of the specific uses of mind maps are as tools for studying, writing, brainstorming, decision-making, problem-solving, project management, planning, and presentation.

CHOOSE YOUR OWN MAP

FIND THE RIGHT MAP THAT FITS YOUR NEEDS AND LEARNING STYLES

A Photo Of Ice Cream [1]

Ice cream is the one thing that every child aged two to 92 enjoys. American presidents, including George Washington, Thomas Jefferson, Abraham Lincoln, Ronald Reagan, and, of course, Joe Biden, were (and are) known to be ice cream fanatics, each with their favorite flavor. [2] George W. Bush's favorite flavor is pralines and cream, which also happens to be among the best-selling Baskin-Robbins flavors. [3]

Everybody knows Baskin-Robbins as the ice cream maker with "31 different flavors." The company came up with the idea of having "31®" flavors to represent a different flavor for each day of the month. The company's flavor library actually exceeds more than 1,400, to suit every possible taste in the ice cream devotee's flavor universe. [4]

Imagine if there were only one ice cream flavor, say, vanilla. The collective reaction would immediately be "Boring!" probably even among vanilla lovers. Everything good can become great if it has variety. Having different types of one thing increases its adaptability for different occasions and needs while enhancing its appeal to its users.

The same thing is true of mind maps. The preceding sections show us mostly spider maps (with a central theme and topics branching out). This is the most popular form of mind map, but there are other types that we should be familiar with to better present our concepts and ideas. Other types include flow maps, system maps, dialogue maps, brace maps, and circle maps. [5]

Flow Map

The term "flow map" is neither new nor exclusively applied to mind maps. In cartography, a flow map is "a map that visualizes movement between places." [6] A flow mind map organizes information in such a way as to convey a sequence. For example, our problem-solving mind map, shown in Chapter 6 as a spider and a tree diagram, has been reconfigured into a flow map and is shown below.

Flow Mind Map

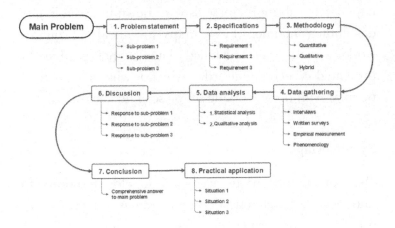

Which of the three types of mapping (spider, tree, or flow map) is best suited for the problem-solving theme and its sub-topics? The answer is: the choice of type depends upon the purpose for which the mind map is intended. The spider and tree diagrams would be ideal for situations where the labor is divided among different individuals or groups, or if different parts of the process may be done simultaneously out of the sequence order (although the sequence is suggested by the numbers assigned to the sub-topics). The flow map above suggests, with its arrowed lines, that a strict linear sequence must be followed because there are no arrows pointing out of sequence. Any revisions to be made will have to come after the last element (step 8, practical applications) is finished, and will have to follow the order indicated by the flow diagram.

Flow maps may be rendered vertically as well as horizontally, depending upon the available space on paper. The sub-topics may also be shown in ascending or descending manner. Flow maps are ideal if you are working with several detailed datasets that need to be presented in a coherent order, which is why they are most popular with those working in the scientific fields.

System Map

"System" is a word often used but seldom thoroughly understood. A system is a group of things, usually a set of procedures or principles, that work together in an organized framework and according to an established method. It is the root word for the word "systematic," which denotes that a process is done in a highly organized and coherent manner.

A system necessarily involves many interconnected components; thus, a system map, which visually represents a system, is one of the most complex types of mind maps. It shows the interrelationships among the various elements, therefore, the lines of a system map do not all radiate from the central theme but may move in various directions.

Below is the mind map of how the strategic management system of an organization functions.

System Mind Map For Strategic Management

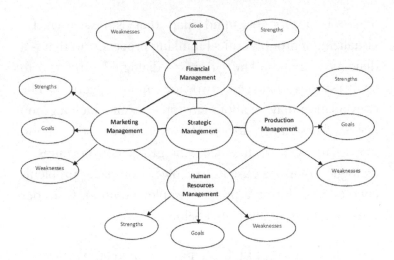

Strategic management involves the goal-setting functions of the organization. Strategic managers scan the environment for threats and opportunities and weigh the relative strengths and weaknesses of the organization. They then set the organization's long-term goals and conceptualize the means and methods by which those goals may be attained.

For this reason, strategic management encompasses all the other subsystems in the organization, such as production and operations, finance, marketing, and human resources. The other subsystems also interact with each other – thus, the lines that connect them, and the outward-directed arrows lead to internal determinations of strengths, weaknesses, and goals important to the organization's strategy.

Dialogue Map

There is a type of mind map that is best used for visualizing a group's critical thinking process, and that is a dialogue map. The term "dialogue" refers to conversations between two or more people. The conversation may be about any topic about which a group needs to exchange ideas. However, while other mind maps can be tools to document group conversations, a dialogue map is used to solve complex problems encountered during a project's implementation. Consider the dialogue map illustrated below.

Dialogue Mind Map For Promoting Skills Trades

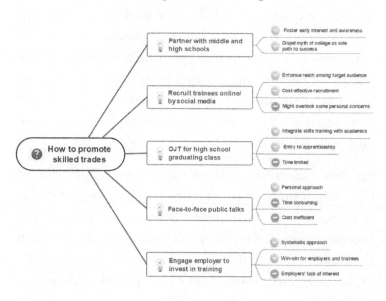

The online version of a dialogue map is an effective problem-solving and communications tool linking team members, managers, and expert advisors working on a project. The project goal for the dialogue map above is to identify programs for promoting skilled trades. Five activities comprise the shortlist suggested by the project team during their dialogue, which became the "lightbulb" topics in the mind map. During the discussion for each activity, the benefits and drawbacks were recorded as "plus" and "minus" twigs linked to the corresponding activity branch. The mind map becomes the summary of the salient points of the dialogue among the project team members. It becomes a tool from which they may proceed during their next meeting.

Not all dialogue maps are constructed in this manner. However, since it charts out a dialogue, the items in a dialogue map are those taken up by members of a group. The dialogue map's main usefulness lies in recording and breaking down specific topics discussed in the conversation. The dialogue map should provide members with a clear understanding of important points agreed upon during what may have been a complicated exchange of ideas.

Brace Map

A brace map has a simpler structure than other mind maps because its purpose is to visually portray part-to-whole relationships of physical objects. Braces may appear in the form of brackets that classify or categorize components to their totality, or species to their genus. A brace map of cars is presented in the next diagram.

Brace Mind Map For Categorizing Cars

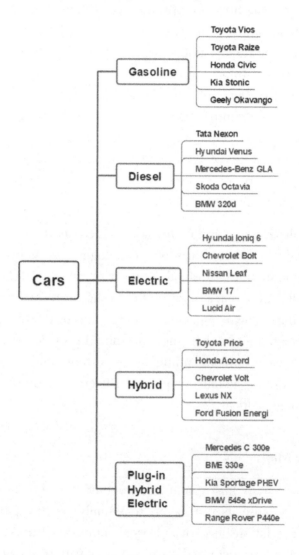

In the brace mind map, the name of the whole object or the more general term is located at the left of the components or more specific objects. The braces signify the levels into which the major part or term is broken down. Brace maps help in the thinking process requiring categorization and organization of things. Brace maps are useful as a tool to enable you to more profoundly understand the nature of things or how they work, such as how a whole is related to its parts, and how its parts are related to its sub-parts.

Circle Map

It is easy to identify a circle map, so-called because it is circular. These types of mind maps are popular because they allow users to see the big picture at one glance. It is useful for presenting important information regarding an event or undertaking as a series of parallel concentric circles within a big circle, and the concentric circles are divided into spokes, each representing an idea, component, or event.

Circle Mind Map Of Foundation Day Activities

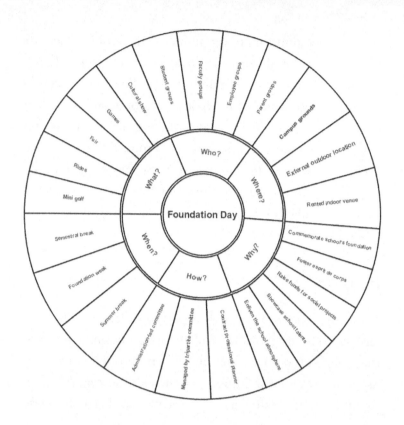

The popular theory is that people are inherently predisposed to learning better through one of our five senses, but we should remember that some scholars regard this as a myth. Nevertheless, many of us prefer learning from mediums that cater to one or two of our senses more than others.

A quick scan of the different types of mind maps underscores their usefulness for individuals who are predominantly visual learners. Mind maps are visual tools, so it is not difficult to conclude that they would appeal greatly to those who learn best by sight. But do they also help other types of learners, and if so, how?

Integrating Mind Maps Into The Different Learning Styles

1. Visual

Research suggests that approximately 65 percent of the general population learn best when they see the information. [7] Visual learners learn directly from the mind maps in a way that auditory and kinesthetic learners will not, thus mind maps provide the greatest benefit to these types of learners. The mind map's effectiveness is further enhanced by using colors and shapes that add to the information content for visual learners.

2. Auditory

Auditory learners comprise 30% of the general population. [8] Mind maps are beneficial for visual learners in a way that they could not be for auditory learners. However, mind maps offer a facility as a tool for auditory learners to arrange their audio files logically and systematically. This enables them to situate their files within a meaningful framework that enhances the efficiency by which they can access their files in the future. Digital mind mapping applications now enable users to embed various types of files within the mind maps created through them

3. Kinesthetic

Visual and auditory learners make up 95% of the general population; the remaining 5% are kinesthetic learners. [9] From the root word kinesthesia which refers to our sense of bodily movement, kinesthetic learners best respond to the movement of their bodies and how they interact with their environment while obtaining information. There are two ways by which mind maps benefit kinesthetic learners. First, mind maps allow learners to express themselves through acts such as drawing, printing, or working on the computer. Second, mind maps help learners remember the information by remembering the movements and pen strokes they used to create the map. [10]

4. Verbal

Unlike visual, aural, and kinesthetic learning, verbal (also known as linguistic) learning is categorized among informational rather than sensory learning styles. There are two types of informational learners – linguistic and mathematical. Information in language form, whether spoken or written, appeals to verbal learners. Information in numerical form or mathematical expressions appeals to mathematical learners. Mind maps appeal to both types of informational learners, particularly if the keywords or notations correspond to the type of information preferred by the learners.

Action Steps

The problem-solving mind map, first shown in Chapter 6 as a spider and a tree diagram, was reconfigured in this chapter as a flow diagram. Which form, if any, do you think is best suited for the problem-solving topic? Does it make a difference which mind map form is used for the same topic? If so, what considerations are useful to determine the best choice of mind map form to use given a particular topic?

Moving On

We have learned about the uses of mind maps and the forms they may assume. Thus far, our examples have been hypothetical or simplistic. In the next chapter, we will apply the lessons so far learned to information gleaned from a complicated piece of academic literature. You met this study in Chapter 2, although it might not have made much sense to you when you first encountered it. We will revisit it in the next chapter and apply the mind mapping technique to understand it better.

Key Takeaways

1. Mind maps come in several forms.

- *Flow maps trace the sequence of steps in a process.*
- *System maps describe the complex interrelationships among elements in a system.*

- *Dialogue maps are visualization tools of a group's thinking process.*
- *Brace maps illustrate the hierarchy of related categories using braces.*
- *Circle maps are circular in design, divided into sections and layers by spokes and concentric circles, and the interrelated elements are located in the sections.*

2. Mind maps support different sensory learning styles in different ways.

- *Majority of the general population are visual learners who benefit the most from mind maps.*
- *Auditory learners benefit from using mind maps to create frameworks for organizing and embedding their audio files.*
- *Kinesthetic learners benefit by remembering either their acts while drawing and printing mind maps, or the movements and pen strokes they used to create the maps.*

3. Mind maps also support informational learning styles. Whether the mind map users be linguistic or mathematical learners, they benefit from the keywords or notations used in the map that correspond to their type of information preference.

8

PREPARATION, EXECUTION, AND INTERPRETATION
A UNIQUE LOOK AT THE BRAIN'S CATEGORIZATION PROCESS

The story and picture below were posted in a Viber chat group. [1]

Our six-year-old handed us a note. His teacher had called my wife and me in for an emergency meeting. We asked our son if he had any idea why, and he said, "She didn't like a drawing I did."

We went in the next day. His teacher pulled out the drawing below and said, "I asked him to draw his family, and he drew this. Would you mind explaining?"

"Not at all," my wife said. "Family vacation. Snorkeling off the Bahamas." 😂😂😂

The teacher must have certainly been embarrassed upon learning of the family's explanation of the drawing. Given the circumstances, though, her interpretation is quite understandable. Some viewers may see this picture as a family of smokers. Others may interpret it as something more bizarre.

Pictures or other graphic works drawn from the imagination tend to convey different meanings. Unlike mathematical charts and graphs, they are not governed by conventional rules or standards that would guide users to the creator's thoughts. Mind maps are pictures that do not follow a set of standards. They are intuitively created and interpreted, a trait that is both an advantage and a disadvantage depending on the viewer's perspective. In this chapter, we will undertake a mind mapping exercise involving just one of many possible methods and outcomes.

Mind Mapping The Brain's Categorization Process

In Chapter 2, we became acquainted with some of the brain's workings, specifically the way it categorizes, remembers, and recalls information from memory. In describing these processes, we were introduced to the parts of the brain and their functions, using scientific terms that are unfamiliar to most people, including us. The long paragraphs may have been difficult to understand, which may leave most of us with a vague understanding of the information conveyed.

This situation provides us with a good opportunity to use mind maps as a tool for the comprehension of complex information.

Let us focus on the categorization process. Making a mind map out of this can be done in many ways, but let us select a method familiar to many. Most students would first resort to outlining the lesson in a way that breaks down the salient parts into a hierarchy of topics and subtopics. A reading of this part in Chapter 2 can be reduced to the following outline.

Outline: The Categorization Process

1. Neocortex

1.1. The largest part of the cerebral cortex

1.2. Responsible for higher-order brain functions including

1.2.1. Cognition

1.2.2. Sensory perception

1.2.3. Generation of motor commands

1.2.4. Spatial reasoning

1.2.5. Language

1.2.6. Decision-making

1.2.7. Emotive-cognitive processes

1.3. Sensory modalities – relay the outside stimuli into the brain by engaging distinct sensory areas that route information to association areas. [2]

1.3.1. Visual – sight

1.3.2. Auditory – hearing

1.3.3. Somatosensory – localized sensations such as pressure, pain, or warmth

1.3.4. Olfactory – smell

1.3.5. Gustatory – taste

1.4. Prefrontal Cortex (PFC)

1.4.1. Modified more by experience

1.4.2. Receives highly processed information from the forebrain and synthesizes them into abstract rule-based categorical distinctions

1.5. Parietal Cortex (PC)

1.5.1. Emphasizes visuospatial functions

1.5.1.1. Visuospatial functions relate to the visual perceptions of the spatial relationships of objects

1.5.2. Link information from the senses with the potentially appropriate response

1.6. Premotor cortex (PMC)

1.6.1. Involved in selecting plans for voluntary movements

1.6.2. Familiar classifications enable plasticity to send stronger signals to PMC than PFC

1.7. Motor cortex (MC)

1.7.1. Involved in the execution of planned voluntary movements

2. Hippocampus

2.1. Plays a major role in learning and memory

2.2. Remembers details of specific experiences and integrates information across events to generalize knowledge

2.3. Episodic inference – allows the memory of past and current events to be combined, thus combining knowledge from both episodes and forming a category

3. Medial temporal lobe (MTL)

3.1. Home to the hippocampi

3.2. Specialized for rapid learning of individual events

3.3. Information acquired from MTL can be transferred to new situations, thus aiding in grouping different bits of information under a common category

4. Basal ganglia

4.1. Located below the cortex

4.2. Primary role is to interact with the sensory modalities in the cortex to process the information in the stimuli

4.3. Generalization is achieved by merging cortical information onto the striatum and other mechanisms involving the basal ganglia

4.4. Performs the following categorization tasks

4.4.1. Trial and error prototype learning – stimuli are formed as distortions of a prototype stimulus

4.4.2. Information integration learning – stimuli are grouped based on an abstract feature

4.4.3. Probabilistic classification – multiple independent features are correlated to identify membership in a particular category

4.4.4. Arbitrary categorization tasks – stimuli in each group do not share any identifiable common characteristics, thus the category membership of each must be independently learned

5. Corticostriatal loops

5.1. Multiple independent neural networks

5.2. Regulatory circuits of the brain that link the cortex with the subcortical regions, including basal ganglia

5.3. Filter and selectively identify stimuli on which the brain bases its cognitive and behavioral responses

5.4. Maintains separation among the different types of stimuli

5.4.1. Visual corticostriatal loop – visual stimulus processing

5.4.2. Motor corticostriatal loop – response selection

5.4.3. Executive and motivational loops – perform tasks in processing feedback and reward

6. Reward and reinforcement

6.1. Midbrain dopaminergic system (Dopamine or DA)

6.1.1. Dopamine

6.1.1.1. A type of neurotransmitter made in the body to produce good feelings

6.1.1.2. Sent by the nervous system to send messages between nerve cells

6.1.1.3. Enables feelings of pleasure, satisfaction, and motivation

6.1.2. DA plays an important role in RL

6.1.2.1. DA neurons provide a mechanism that modifies synapses

6.1.2.2. Synapses are the narrow spaces between neurons

6.1.2.3. Synaptic modification creates the mechanisms for memory and learning

6.1.2.4. Enables a particular type of RL underlying human and animal behavior

6.2. Reinforcement learning (RL) mechanisms

6.2.1. Adaptive processes by which an animal uses its previous experience to improve the outcomes of future choices

6.2.2. An animal chooses its actions according to how much future reward it may expect from each action

6.2.3. Computations theory provides a useful model for understanding how much reward is expected based on experience.

<u>End Of Outline</u>

The outline is one step in reducing the material into manageable parts, but as it is, it remains formidable and difficult to understand. Next, let us convert the outline into a mind map in the same manner we arrived at the Japanese History Mind Map from the Timeline of Japanese History in <u>Chapter 5</u>. (Here we see how breaking down paragraphs of information into tables helps our outlines arrive at topics we could assign in a mind map.) The outline can be rendered into the following mind map.

The Categorization Process Mind Map

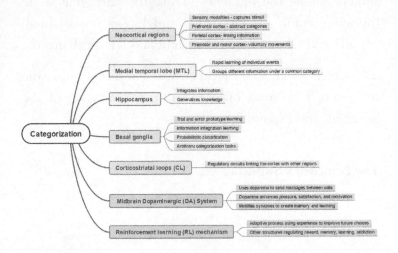

How did we arrive at the mind map above? Looking at the outline, we notice how the functions are organized around the main physical parts of the brain, which are the outline's numbered topics. These are the neocortex, medial temporal lobe, hippocampus, basal ganglia, corticostriatal loops, dopaminergic system, and reinforcement learning mechanisms that comprise the initial branches that emanate from the central topic.

Following these outline topics are the subtopics that may be categorized as descriptions of the physical part, its components, or its functions. These subtopics are then linked to the initial branches on our mind map in their abbreviated or summary form.

In further discussions within the material, certain parts of the brain are closely related to each other. In the mind map, these close relationships are denoted by colors shared among the branches. Thus, the parts that share the same color are the MTL and hippocampus, basal ganglia and CL, and the DA system and RL mechanism.

The canvas has begun to feel crowded at this point, so the next step is to break off into sub-maps for each of the branches and expand from there.

The Neocortex Sub-Map

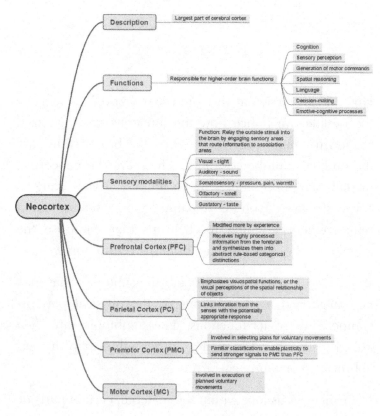

The neocortex, also known as the neocortical region, comprises the sensory modalities, PFC, PC, PMC, and MC, each of which have their descriptions and functions attached as twigs to the branch. Aside from its parts, the neocortex also has its own description and function which are attached to the sub-map's central theme. This mind map expounds on one small part of the main map. It enables us to comprehend with one glance the various components of this region of the brain, and how they are distinct from yet operate in conjunction with each other. This branch and its sub-branches are assigned the color green to distinguish them from the other branches.

The Hippocampus And The Medial Temporal Lobe Sub-Map

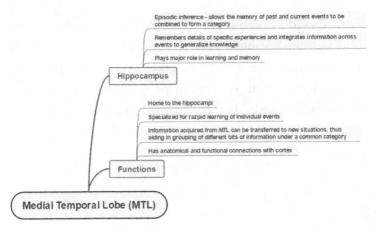

The MTL and hippocampus are the two branches coded yellow on the main map. However, in the sub-map, they are combined in the single topic MTL with the hippocampus forming only a branch. Why so? This is because the notes explain that the hippocampus is physically located within the medial temporal lobe. In the main map, the hippocampus was assigned its own branch because of its specialized functions that transcend its designation as a mere part of the MTL.

Many people will look at this and say that this sub-map is not right. It does not follow the rule that each branch should form a main topic in the sub-map. Here is where the mind mapping technique shows its versatility. As mentioned in Chapter 4, mind maps have no conventions or standards. Creating a mind map is intuitive. The map's interpretation rests in the mind of its creator, therefore, as long as the creator's purposes are met, the map is useful and valid.

From the MTL sub-map, we could interpret this as the hippocampus, being a part of the MTL, plays a role in the latter's more general functions. Aside from that, the hippocampus also performs more specialized categorization tasks that are shown in its sub-branches.

The Basal Ganglia And The Corticostriatal Loops Sub-Map

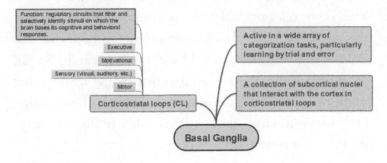

The next component in the main map is the basal ganglia, but as we can see from the figure above, included in the sub-map of the basal ganglia is another component of the main map, the corticostriatal loops. Here is a case that is similar to that of the MTL and hippocampus. In the main map, the basal ganglia and the corticostriatal loops are separate branches. However, a close analysis of the source material reveals that the corticostriatal loops are intricately connected with all the regions under the cortex, including the basal ganglia. For categorization, the corticostriatal loops and basal ganglia are functionally integrated, and their inclusion in the same sub-map supports this interpretation.

The Midbrain Dopaminergic System And The Reinforcement Learning Mechanisms Sub-Map

The next sub-map once again shows the close workings of the last two branches of the main map, the midbrain dopaminergic system and the reinforcement learning (RL) mechanisms. A careful reading of the original material shows that reinforcement learning as a function of the brain is not relegated solely to the midbrain dopaminergic system. Knowledge about most of the workings of the brain is still being developed by current research. So far, RL mechanisms are dispersed across many areas of the brain, but what is certain is that the release of dopamine (DA) plays a large part in how the brain associates rewards with certain behaviors.

The mind map below describes reward-based learning concerning categorization. If new knowledge from stimuli is linked to an existing category or forms a new category, learning is created. If the behavior response to it is rewarded by the pleasurable sensation created by the release of dopamine to the nerve cell, the learning is reinforced. When a similar situation is once more encountered, the behavior is repeated, which triggers more dopamine release. The synapses where learning is stored are strengthened, and soon the behavioral response time to similar future stimuli is shortened due to rapid learning.

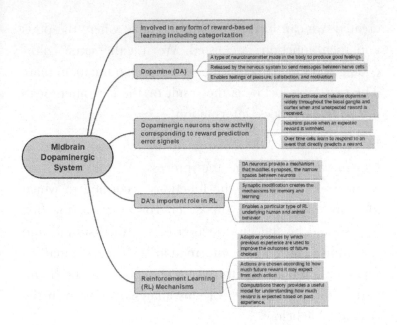

The sub-maps of the brain's physical components are helpful to us in understanding and memorizing their functions. However, merely identifying the components may be too fragmented if we wish to comprehend the categorization process as a system. We need to take the material a step further by viewing the components holistically, starting with the stimuli and ending with the new knowledge categorized and memorized.

Analyzing The Categorization Flow

Remember how we organized the original material by creating an outline to focus on the components? We could employ another technique to condense the material to analyze the process. With the main map and sub-maps we created, we can form the following table where the parts and their functions are listed. We use the same color-coding scheme to anchor their presence on the main map. The first table below is the result of the first attempt to integrate the process information.

In the first table, the column at the left was created to sequence the steps in the process. We assigned the numbers by analyzing the functions according to which logically comes before the other. For instance, the first step should be the introduction of outward stimuli into the brain. The sensory information is then regulated, or separated, and moved to the lower regions of the brain, and so forth. The result of this analysis is shown in the second table below.

First Table

	Process	Mechanism	Part of brain
1	Outside stimuli are relayed into the brain	Distinct sensory areas are engaged to route information to association areas	Sensory modalities: Visual, auditory, somatosensory, olfactory, gustatory, etc.
5	Higher processed information is received from forebrain and synthesized into abstract, rule-based categorical distinctions	Modification by experience	Prefrontal cortex (PFC)
3	Information from the senses is linked to the potentially appropriate response	Emphasis on visuospatial functions; close functional link with the PFC	Parietal cortex
10	Selecting plans for voluntary movements (categorical responses)	Familiar classifications enable plasticity to send stronger signals to PMC rather than PFC	Premotor cortex (PMC)
11	Execution of planned voluntary movements	Reliance on motor systems increases (and decreases for other systems) as expertise develops for familiar classifications	Primary motor cortex (MC)
6	Episodic inference – the memory and knowledge of past and current events are combined to form a category	Remembers details of specific experiences and integrates information across events to form generalized knowledge	Hippocampus
7	Rapid learning of events	Information from MTL is transferred to new situations, thus aiding the grouping of different bits of information under a common category	Medial temporal lobe (MTL)
4	Sensory information processing; generalization involving cortical information	Interacts with sensory modalities to process the information • Trial and error prototype learning • Information integration learning • Probabilistic classification • Arbitrary categorization tasks	Basal ganglia
2	Regulates information between the cortex and subcortical regions	Filter, selectively identify, and maintain separation among the different types of stimuli: • Visual CL – visual stimuli processing • Motor CL – response selection • Executive & motivation CL – processing feedback and reward	Corticostriatal loops (CL)
8	Synaptic modification to create mechanisms for memory and learning	DA neurons provides mechanism that modifies synapses, enable feelings of pleasure, satisfaction, and motivation	Midbrain dopaminergic system (DA)
9	Brain uses previous experience to improve the outcome of future choices	Future actions are chosen according to how much future reward may be expected from the action	Reinforcement learning mechanisms (RL)

Second Table

	Process	Mechanism	Part of brain
1	Outside stimuli are relayed into the brain	Distinct sensory areas are engaged to route information to association areas	Sensory modalities: Visual, auditory, somatosensory, olfactory, gustatory, etc.
2	Regulates information between the cortex and subcortical regions	Filter, selectively identify, and maintain separation among the different types of stimuli: • Visual CL – visual stimuli processing • Motor CL – response selection • Executive & motivation CL – processing feedback and reward	Corticostriatal loops (CL)
3	Information from the senses is linked to the potentially appropriate response	Emphasis on visuospatial functions; close functional link with the PFC	Parietal cortex
4	Sensory information processing; generalization involving cortical information	Interacts with sensory modalities to process the information • Trial and error prototype learning • Information integration learning • Probabilistic classification • Arbitrary categorization tasks	Basal ganglia
5	Higher processed information is received from forebrain and synthesized into abstract, rule-based categorical distinctions	Modification by experience	Prefrontal cortex (PFC)
6	Episodic inference – the memory and knowledge of past and current events are combined to form a category	Remembers details of specific experiences and integrates information across events to form generalized knowledge	Hippocampus
7	Rapid learning of events	Information from MTL is transferred to new situations, thus aiding the grouping of different bits of information under a common category	Medial temporal lobe (MTL)
8	Synaptic modification to create mechanisms for memory and learning	DA neurons provides mechanism that modifies synapses, enable feelings of pleasure, satisfaction, and motivation	Midbrain dopaminergic system (DA)
9	Brain uses previous experience to improve the outcome of future choices	Future actions are chosen according to how much future reward may be expected from the action	Reinforcement learning mechanisms (RL)
10	Selecting plans for voluntary movements (categorical responses)	Familiar classifications enable plasticity to send stronger signals to PMC rather than PFC	Premotor cortex (PMC)
11	Execution of planned voluntary movements	Reliance on motor systems increases (and decreases for other systems) as expertise develops for familiar classifications	Primary motor cortex (MC)

Why is this part of the analysis necessary? Our purpose is to understand a process, and this necessarily involves the sequence of steps that describe the process. While we do this, we should remember that we are simplifying the material being learned, so it may somewhat lack accuracy. Much like learning to ride a bike, we would expect to fall a few times at first. Digesting the lesson takes many incremental stages, each moving us forward in our understanding.

After the second table, we are now ready to create a flow type of mind map which we were introduced to in Chapter 7. Following the sequence of steps, we arrive at the following diagram.

The Categorization Flow Diagram

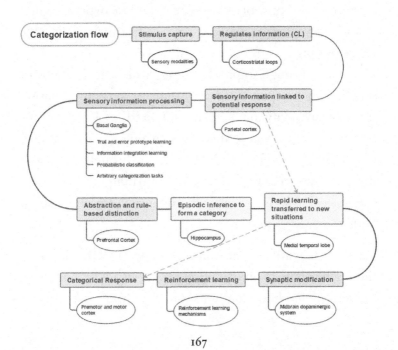

The process begins with the introduction of the outside stimulus by our sensory modalities. Corticostriatal loops separate the information according to the sensory type involved and convey the impulse to the parietal cortex, where the information is linked to a potential response. However, particularly if the information is new, it undergoes a longer process in the basal ganglia, which "learns" through four methods: trial and error (distortion of a prototype), information integrating (grouped according to abstract feature), probabilistic classification (independent features are compared), or arbitrary categorization (absence of common traits).

Based on this learning, a rule is abstracted and a rule-based distinction is formed, likely within the prefrontal cortex. This new episode is integrated with knowledge gathered from previous experiences and incorporated into a category, or a new category is formed in the hippocampus. The learning extracted is applied to new situations through rapid learning, while simultaneously sent to the dopaminergic system to modify synapses through plasticity (i.e., adaptation and molding of the neurons to incorporate the new learning). The release of dopamine reinforces learning through various mechanisms. Finally, the new learning is used for categorical responses through the premotor and motor cortex.

There is a winding path among the topics that denotes the regular flow of information processing. There is also a broken green line that cuts directly from the sensory information to rapid learning to categorical response. Steps involving detailed categorization, inference, and abstraction are bypassed. The actual mechanism may be more complex, or there may be multiple mechanisms that have the same result, but the implication is the same. Information is diverted around the more complex process steps when the episode has been previously encountered and categorized, so the appropriate behavior is more quickly carried out.

Let's see how this works with an example. Jack visits a Korean restaurant for the first time. He orders a dish called *ramyeon* which he is thoroughly unfamiliar with. When it is served, he sees that it has broth, noodles, vegetables, some meat, and a hard-boiled egg. His brain absorbs these visual stimuli, and since Jack has previously eaten ramen at a Japanese restaurant, he expects that it might taste like ramen (distorted prototype learning).

Jack dips his spoon in the broth and realizes that it has a less robust taste than ramen broth. As Jack eats, the taste and smell information, relayed separately from the visual information, notes the similarities and differences with ramen. From what would have been a complete categorization of *ramyeon* as ramen, his mind abstracts that there are some "common rules" (noodles, soup, egg) and some "differentiated rules" (less robust, spicier). Based on whether Jack experiences pleasure or not from this new dish, Jack may return for more (reinforced learning) or not at all.

If Jack likes his first experience with *ramyeon* and decides to return, this first encounter would have taught him what to expect, and his reactions to repeated episodes will not take the long route to process new information. Instead, he will immediately consume the *ramyeon* with familiarity and may not even compare it to the Japanese ramen, which he will regard as a similar but also distinctly different experience.

Action Steps

In this chapter, we interpreted the section in Chapter 2 that described the brain's categorization function and arrived at several mind maps that simplified the process. Are the mind maps faithful representations of the section? A careful comparison would show that they hew close to the original material. But are they accurate? As their creator, I admit I am not a medical doctor and there may have been some inaccuracies. After all, the full scope of the brain's physiology is not covered by the source, an academic study by Seger and Miller. [3]

Much like the drawing of the family snorkeling off the Bahamas, the mind maps in this chapter are my interpretation. Though they may be flawed, this does not diminish their usefulness to me. As I gain more knowledge, I may improve upon them. Some of you, readers, may have a more thorough knowledge of the brain's functionality, or upon reading the source, you may have a better interpretation of it. What improvements can you make in the mind maps presented?

You could also try to mind map the shorter section in Chapter 2 that describes how the brain stores information. You can look up the source material, or other research if you want. Understanding scientific discussions is a challenge, but trying to mind map these complicated discussions will give you a better feel of the true power of mind mapping.

Moving On

Mind mapping the brain's functions is a daunting exercise. Drawing the mind maps would have posed more challenges and resulted in hand-drawn diagrams that would fall short of publication standards. For this book, the mind maps were drawn with the invaluable help of the digital software EdrawMind©. [4] Many mind mapping applications are available online to make the drawing task easier and more presentable. Turn the page to discover some of the more popular mind mapping app brands.

Key Takeaways

1. Pictures or images that are purely creations of the imagination are variously interpreted depending upon the viewers' perception. Only the creator could accurately state the meaning of the image.
2. Information that is difficult to comprehend because of its complexity, such as a discussion on the brain's mechanisms, can be processed into

notes in an outline or a table where the information remains in verbal form, and then into mind maps.

3. Several mind maps can be created from the same information, using different forms such as spider maps and flow maps, to support different nuances by which the same information can be perceived.

4. When the mind encounters new stimuli, it links this with previous knowledge in long-term memory and responds accordingly. The brain responds more swiftly to frequently encountered stimuli because it bypasses processes undertaken for new or unfamiliar stimuli.

9

MIND MAPPING FOR THE MODERN TIMES

EXPLORE THE ADVANCED FEATURES OF DIGITAL MIND MAPPING

" At the end of the day, the two of the three highest human desires are the desire to be useful, and the desire to share stories. We have been doing both since our distant ancestors sat around a savanna campfire sharing their days and their dreams. Now, thanks to digital media, the circle around the campfire has grown to encompass (if we wish) all of humanity." – Paul Saffo, Stanford University Professor, on the ubiquitousness of digital connectivity. [1]

As a peer math tutor to my classmates in high school, one of the greatest challenges I contended with was guiding my classmates in geometry and trigonometry – over the phone. The year was 1976, and before our major exams, I would get eleventh-hour phone calls from members of my tutorial group about solving problems in these subjects. But geometry and trigonometry solutions are highly graphical, and telephones then were audio-only devices.

The challenge lay in verbally describing hand-drawn solutions involving angles, triangles, and other geometric forms. This required "transcribing" the pictures in my head into the head of whoever I was tutoring at that moment. The task was not easy. My listener would frequently "see" a different image from what I was describing, further muddling an already difficult conversation. It was a wiedy process, but in the end, the job was accomplished with much time, patience, and mental calisthenics.

Today, sending visual information across great distances and in real time is an integral part of daily life. An image can be sent accurately and instantaneously to millions of people, thanks to the power of modern digital technology. Cybernetics has revolutionized multimodal communications, adding a new dimension to mind mapping's already formidable versatility.

Digital Mind Mapping Features

While the early programs were broadly divergent, nearly all the mind mapping applications widely used today share similar features. Through the years, developers responded to meet the demands of the public, and their products now incorporate those capabilities that provide users with the greatest utility.

Generally, mind mapping software allows for several ways by which a mind map's complexity can be reduced. [2] For instance, some branches not currently in use may be closed. Collapsing a branch makes it disappear from view together with its sub-topics. Instead, a symbol such as a plus (+) sign replaces the collapsed branch. Clicking the plus sign brings the hidden branch into view again, ready for use.

Alternatively, you could focus only on a branch and its twigs by closing off the rest of the map. The branch topic appears as the central topic of the mind map, and you have a smaller mind map that you can concentrate on. When you are done examining the branch, you can open the larger mind map once more to see the branch in relation to the other topics.

Some of the map's contents can also be filtered or hidden. Mind mapping programs allow you to hide parts of your map by applying a filter based on the criteria you specify. When the filter is removed, the hidden contents reappear in the mind map. In this manner, you can manage the amount of information on your mind map as they are needed by turning off task data, notes, icons, hyperlinks, or specific search items.

Finally, you can use the mind map program to divide a large, complicated map into several smaller linked maps. Topics that have an abundance of details compared to others are good candidates to become linked maps. When the command to create linked maps is used, the topic remains in the main map, but a copy of the branch and its details are stored in a separate mind map to which you can quickly navigate from the main map, and vice-versa.

Communication And Collaboration

One of the outstanding features that current mind mapping applications have over traditional and early digital mind mapping is their ability to facilitate remote communication and collaboration among several users in real time, whether they be teams working together in brainstorming or planning sessions, or teachers and students engaged in blended or remote learning.

The conditions imposed during the pandemic lockdowns during 2020-2022 in various parts of the world, characterized by isolation and lack of mobility, underscore the urgency of remote communication and collaboration. Communication must be multimodal, combining verbal, visual, and kinetic (conveying motion by digital impulses) exchange. Collaboration is characterized by real-time interaction that makes possible the exchange of ideas and feedback on them.

Manual mind mapping, using paper or a physical whiteboard, is a great technique for face-to-face communication and collaboration. Digital technology exponentially magnifies mind mapping's inherent potential by transcending distance and time constraints. The degree to which ready-made templates and other aids have been developed complements the tool's connectivity. For this reason, collaboration and communication features have become a standard feature in current mind mapping applications.

Some Of Today's Best Mind Mapping Software

While most mind mapping applications share common features, users have gravitated toward products that they prefer over others. Seven software brands are presented here, together with their consumer ratings and descriptions. The scores were derived from GetApp®, a website that gathers customers' reviews of various software applications. The rankings are based jointly on the scores and the number of reviews garnered by each product.

For this listing, only positive reviews have been gathered, since negative reviews may point to weaknesses that the product developer may address in time and may, therefore, no longer be relevant. Readers are encouraged to visit the websites cited and other reviews before selecting products that they may want to try out. All products mentioned offer a free trial version or a trial period, with options to purchase beyond the period or if additional features are desired. [3]

Software #1: Miro

GetApp Overall rating: 4.7/5 (1.2K)

Miro [4] is an online collaborative whiteboard platform that provides support for remote teams to work together effectively in real time. It is a robust tool for brainstorming with digital sticky notes, concept mapping, presentations, and planning and managing agile workflows. Team members can discuss projects and ideas in board chats, leave tagged comments, and use voice and video calls. Miro's features include presentation mode, seamless communication, real-time collaboration, infinite canvas, timer, and templates library. Moreover, Miro is very user-friendly and requires no learning curve since it is as simple as a whiteboard, making it easy to onboard new team members into existing workflows. It accommodates texts, docs, images, videos, wireframes, and other media. Miro allows users to see the big picture of projects, and if they wish to see the details, all they need to do is zoom in on the relevant areas.

Software #2: Lucidspark

GetApp Overall Rating: 4.7/5 (353)

Lucidspark [5] is a virtual whiteboard that helps remote teams collaborate. Launched in 2020, it is produced by a Utah-based software company co-founded by Ben Dilts and Karl Sun called Lucid Software, Inc. Lucid Software prides itself in being a leader in visual communication with a host of Lucidspark-compatible products such as Lucidchart and Lucidscale. Lucid's products benefit over 60 million users worldwide. Its customers include companies such as Google, GE, NBC Universal, and a host of 500 Fortune companies. Lucid's partners include Google, Atlassian, Microsoft, and several industry leaders. [6]

Lucidspark's features include integrations, infinite canvas, sticky notes, freehand drawing, chat, templates, timer, voting, and others. Lucidspark allows teams not only to brainstorm but take their ideations to the next level by organizing those ideas to drive action. These capabilities include assisted grouping and Lucidchart import/export that help users develop ideas from notes and scribbles into actionable plans and strategies. Lucidspark is a part of the Lucid collaboration suite, so far the only visual collaboration suite for teams. Ideas that begin with Lucidspark can seamlessly transfer to Lucidchart and Lucidchart Cloud Insights until the full project lifecycle is completed and ideas are transformed into reality. [7]

Software #3: MindMeisters

GetApp Overall Rating: 4.7/5 (270)

MindMeister is a web-based, online mind mapping software that enables its users to visualize, share, and present their ideas via the cloud. It was launched in 2007 by MeisterLabs GmbH in Bayern, Germany by the company's founders, Michael Hollauf and Till Vollmer. One decade after its launch, the software has more than six million users worldwide [8] and is still very popular today.

There are many features MindMaster has incorporated into its platform. The essential features include expertly designed themes, mixed map layouts, and professional presentations. It also has predefined templates, key shortcuts, and connections between mind maps. Its styling options include individual topic styling, line styling, tintable images and emojis, freely-positioned topics, and Markdown syntax for mind map topics, comments, and notes. Among its advanced features are the outline mode, focus mode, expandable notes, attachments, and imports in the form of conversions from other platforms such as MindManager, XMind, and Freemind, among others. MindMeister has collaboration features for brainstorming and version history, as well as integrations and embedded media. [9]

Software #4: Cacoo

GetApp Overall rating: 4.7/5 (146)

Cacoo is a web-based tool that is great for people who are not particularly technology-savvy. It is a user-friendly mind map maker with a connector button that enables users to quickly create shapes to expand their ideas. It can work with images, data notes, and charts which makes it ideal for note-taking and brainstorming sessions, whether in a home or office setting. Cacoo employs an intuitive interface and ready-made shapes and templates with automatic line connectors. Its plus features include multiple user access in simultaneously editing the diagrams; chat, comment, or video chat capability inside the tool; hundreds of templates to get the user started; and ease in sharing and exporting diagrams in SVG, PDF, PowerPoint, and PostScript. [10] Cacoo also enables presenting and sharing users' work via its presentation mode, screen share, shared folders, public diagram links, and embeddable diagram viewer. In addition, it organizes and stores the mind maps in shared project folders, employing team management, security settings, groups for easy access, and guest access features. [11]

Software #5: LiquidText

GetApp Overall Rating: 4.7/5 (114)

LiquidText is software that differs from the digital mind mapping apps that describe themselves as virtual whiteboards. It is, firstly, a document analysis tool. It captures texts, readings, notes, highlights, annotations, and observations like paper, but goes a step further to link them to source materials and each other. Organized notes and excerpts can be exported in standard formats so they can be shared and communicated to others. LiquidText documents and maps these materials in a form that is clear and shareable. [12] It streamlines and integrates creating a mind map from PDF sources. [13]

How LiquidText differs from the other mind mapping apps is how it works from raw material. Users combine multiple readings into one workspace as well as pull out excerpts from different documents. LiquidText then seamlessly integrates them in a mind map, outline, or combination style. By clicking on the excerpt, the user is transported to the section of the reading where the excerpt is found, allowing the user to read it. The software also has highlighting as well as drawing and annotating functions. These functions facilitate students' absorption of reading-heavy lessons. Exporting the file as a PDF greatly helps users prepare for their exams. It can be integrated with Dropbox, Google Drive, iCloud, email, and other storage and communication modes. [14]

Software # 6: Padlet

GetApp Overall rating: 4.8/5(76)

Padlet is a digitized notice board primarily aimed at enhancing education communications. Its primary purpose is to create a space for teachers and students to share notes, thoughts, and discussions. Its improvement over a physical notice board is that it allows the use of rich media, including words, images, documents, audio, videos, and links. Multimedia from other online resources like Drive, One Drive, and others may also be pulled and posted on the walls. It is also real-time, so anyone sharing the space sees the new information as soon as they are posted. Padlet is accessible by almost any device to create single or multiple walls that act as blank slates for any postings the moderator (creator) wants to share with guests. [15]

Padlet allows for a more customized experience for its users by providing a variety of formats. One of these is a mind mapping format called Canvas. This tool allows users to move sticky notes to facilitate the creation of mind maps. Concepts, facts, and thoughts posted on the walls are visually connected by users. In this manner,

Canvas provides them with a way to organize and synthesize the information in their various forms. [16] The Canvas format helps teachers and students collaborate across devices and settings by enabling learners to see how concepts are related. Students visually represent their thinking, and teachers gain insight into how their students comprehend specific concepts without the need for voluminous texts.

Software #7: EdrawMind

GetApp Overall rating: 4.6/5 (51)

EdrawMind (formerly known as MindMaster) is a full-featured collaborative mind mapping and brainstorming digital tool. [17] More than 25 million users, us included, have enjoyed the benefits of both individual and collaborative mind mapping created by Edraw, founded in 2004. It is a cross-platform tool and is available for Windows, MacOS, Linus, Web, Android, and IOS. [18] It has two editions, Free and Business, and its editions since 2021 support at least ten languages – English, Chinese (Simplified and Traditional), French, German, Korean, Japanese, Spanish, Italian, Russian, and Portuguese. In 2020, a new mind map gallery was added to EdrawMind where users can share mind map templates and resources. As of May 31, 2023, EdrawMind gained an upgraded artificial intelligence feature with its One-Click Solution. [19] This new feature is designed to boost speed and efficiency with the following AI features:

- *Edraw AI 2.0 analyzes and interprets the user's information input to provide relevant suggestions and automate the entire mind mapping process.*
- *Multi-level mind maps are generated to create comprehensive mind maps at various levels with just one click.*
- *Enables access to 12 predefined ready-to-use templates for frequently encountered work-life scenarios (e.g., brainstorming, SWOT analysis, text generation) to improve productivity.*
- *Saves time and effort during the annotation process by providing automatic annotation and intelligent suggestions to organize your mind map.*

Other Mind Mapping Software

Numerous other mind mapping applications have gained popularity among users. They include Bubble.us, Celtx, Creately, Coggle, Mindomo, MindManager, Minitab Workspace, PICC Software, and many others. Several of these software applications have garnered GetApp scores equal to, if not higher than, the seven mentioned above. However, they were not included in the list because there were too few (less than 50) respondents who rated and reviewed their performance to date. It is possible that, in due time, many of them may develop further to gain popularity among a wider customer pool. It is also likely that users now may find that one of them caters more to their needs and prefer it to the others listed here.

Action Steps

The mind mapping applications described in this chapter all have free trial versions with their basic features. Try them out and see which are best suited to your purposes. Students and researchers will likely favor LiquidText's document analysis capabilities, while educators conducting blended learning classes will find Padlet's rich multimedia features very useful. You could search online for other applications beyond the seven mentioned here, and you will probably find one to your liking.

Moving On

Digital tools provide numerous benefits for different tasks, and mind mapping is no exception. You will find that most mind mapping software brands are user-friendly to the point that they could help you produce your first professional-looking mind map on your first attempt. Your mind mapping skills could only improve from there.

Key Takeaways

1. Digital technology has enabled the creation of mind mapping platforms that have revolutionized the way we work and study as individuals and groups.
2. Standard digital mind mapping features include design simplification, view control, virtual

expansion, ease of operation, versatility, and compatibility with other data platforms.

3. Remote multipoint communication and collaboration capabilities are necessary and desirable features in the most popular mind mapping software.

4. Some mind mapping software brands have specialized features that enhance their suitability for specific purposes. Users should canvas carefully and take advantage of free trials before purchasing a mind mapping app.

AFTERWORD

"A single neuron in the brain is an incredibly complex machine that even today we don't understand. A single 'neuron' in a neural network is an incredibly simple mathematical function that captures a minuscule fraction of the complexity of a biological neuron." – Andrew Ng [1]

A popular song [2] begins with the phrase, "Lost as a child's first thought." When was it, indeed, that we first began to think, and what must we have thought about? Thoughts are so ephemeral that it takes the brain's mysterious functionalities to capture them and convert them into knowledge. Fleeting thoughts, when not contemplated upon, will truly be lost, like our first thoughts as children.

To capture these thoughts and permanently store them for later retrieval, humans invented external devices that complement our thought processes. Our forebears committed their thoughts to written manuscripts and documents. More recently, computer systems were created to function as artificial brains to complement our human brains. Somewhere in between the manuscripts and machines, mind maps were devised as a repository of our thoughts.

Mind maps correspond to our thoughts as artificial neurons correspond to brain neurons. They are tangible representations of our abstract concepts, simple pictures that stand for complex ideas. In their simplicity, they help us understand, remember, and communicate what we think.

For those of you who were not acquainted with mind maps before reading this book, we hope that these chapters have opened up fresh options for you that will help you in your studies, work, or regular tasks in your daily lives, particularly the introduction to mind mapping software. If you are already familiar with mind mapping, then hopefully, these chapters have helped you review the basic techniques and maybe acquire some new insights into their uses.

If there is anything anybody should take away from this book, these would be the four easy steps to make a mind map in Chapter 5. There is a reason why mind maps are intuitively created. Drawing what we think is an activity even little children do instinctively, such as the child who drew his family on vacation snorkeling in the Bahamas. Since the majority of us are visual thinkers, we have an innate ability to commit to paper (or digital medium) pictures that we see with our mind's eye. Mind maps are just that – fleeting mental images made tangible and permanent for our benefit and that of others.

The next time you feel the need to take notes, clarify a concept, document a plan, communicate an idea more effectively, or simply record flashes of inspired insight during a brainstorming session, don't hesitate. Map it.

Much like trapping the electrical impulse transmitted between neurons, mind maps capture our thoughts and hold them immobilized for all time. Like Porphyry's Tree.

Think about it.

OVER 10,000 PEOPLE HAVE ALREADY SUBSCRIBED. DID YOU TAKE YOUR CHANCE YET?

In general, around 50% of the people who start reading do not finish a book. You are the exception, and we are happy you took the time.

To honor this, we invite you to join our exclusive Wisdom University newsletter. You cannot find this subscription link anywhere else on the web but in our books!

Upon signing up, you'll receive two of our most popular bestselling books, highly acclaimed by readers like yourself. We sell copies of these books daily, but you will receive them as a gift. Additionally, you'll gain access to two transformative short sheets and enjoy complimentary access to all our upcoming e-books, completely free of charge!

This offer and our newsletter are free; you can unsubscribe anytime.

Here's everything you get:

✓ How To Train Your Thinking eBook   **($9.99 Value)**
✓ The Art Of Game Theory eBook   **($9.99 Value)**
✓ Break Your Thinking Patterns Sheet   **($4.99 Value)**
✓ Flex Your Wisdom Muscle Sheet   **($4.99 Value)**
✓ All our upcoming eBooks   **($199.80* Value)**

Total Value: $229.76

Go to wisdom-university.net for the offer!

(Or simply scan the code with your camera)

Scan Me

*If you download 20 of our books for free, this would equal a value of
199.80$

THE TEAM BEHIND WISDOM
UNIVERSITY

Michael Meisner, Founder and CEO

When Michael ventured into publishing books on Amazon, he discovered that his favorite topics - the intricacies of the human mind and behavior - were often tackled in a way that's too complex and unengaging. Thus, he dedicated himself to making his ideal a reality: books that effortlessly inform, entertain, and resonate with readers' everyday experiences, enabling them to enact enduring positive changes in their lives.

Together with like-minded people, this ideal became his passion and profession. Michael is in charge of steering the strategic direction and brand orientation of Wisdom University, as he continues to improve and extend his business.

Claire M. Umali, Publishing Manager

Collaborative work lies at the heart of crafting books, and keeping everyone on the same page is an essential task. Claire oversees all the stages of this collaboration, from researching to outlining and from writing to editing. In her free time, she writes online reviews and likes to bother her cats.

Lorey L. de Guzman-Dadula, Co-Publishing Manager

Lorey is a dedicated writer who shares her home with three cats, one dog, and her beloved husband. In her role as Wisdom University's co-publishing manager, Lorey taps into her prolific professional experience in management and education to effectively support a diverse array of amazing talents at every stage of the publication.

Dianna Aquino, Writer

The author has a doctorate and has taught in college and graduate school for 40 years. Outside the academe, she has had field experience in business management, engineering, law, finance, and marketing. She has been married for 37 years and has raised three children, now professionals in their own right. Her wealth of experience and academic foundation enable this book's grounded approach through straightforward explanations and everyday examples.

Jevette Brown, Content Editor

Jevette is an editor with a background in copy editing, academic writing, and journalism. With bachelor's degrees in Communications and English and a graduate degree in Legal Studies, Jevette's varied experience provides a valuable perspective for diverse content and audiences. Her priority is helping writers fine-tune their material to display their unique voices best.

Sandra Agarrat, Language Editor

Sandra Wall Agarrat is an experienced freelance academic editor/proofreader, writer, and researcher. Sandra holds graduate degrees in Public Policy and International Relations. Her portfolio of projects includes books, dissertations, theses, scholarly articles, and grant proposals.

Michelle Olarte, Researcher

Michelle conducts extensive research and constructs thorough outlines that substantiate Wisdom University's book structure. She graduated from Communication Studies with high honors. Her works include screenplays, book editing, book advertisements, and magazine articles.

Ralph Escarda, Layout Designer

Ralph's love for books prevails in his artistic preoccupations. He is an avid reader of non-fictional books and an advocate of self-improvement through education. He dedicates his spare time to doing portraits and sports.

Jemarie Gumban, Publishing Assistant

Jemarie is in charge of thoroughly examining and evaluating the profiles and potential of the many aspiring writers for Wisdom University. With an academic background in Applied Linguistics and a meaningful experience as an industrial worker, she approaches her work with a discerning eye and fresh outlook. Guided by her unique perspective, Jemarie derives fulfillment from turning a writer's desire to create motivational literature into tangible reality.

Evangeline Obiedo, Publishing Assistant

Evangeline diligently supports our books' journey, from the writing stage to connecting with our readers. Her commitment to detail permeates her work, encompassing tasks such as initiating profile evaluations and ensuring seamless delivery of our newsletters. Her love for learning extends into the real world - she loves traveling and experiencing new places and cultures.

REFERENCES

Introduction

1. Bland, J. (2018). *Figure 17.1 Illustration by Edward Cogger of the anonymous nursery rhyme Hey Diddle Diddle (circa 1885, public domain)* [Illustration]. Learning through literature. In Grafton, S. & Copland, F. (Eds.) *The Routledge Handbook of Teaching English to Young Learners.* Routledge. https://doi.org/10.4324/9781315623672
2. For the biological aspect, see: Ionta, Silvio. (2021). Visual neuropsychology in development: Anatomo-Functional brain mechanisms of action/perception binding in health and disease. *Frontiers in Human Neuroscience, 15.* https://doi.org/10.3389/fnhum.2021.689912
3. Bradford, W. C. (2004). Reaching the visual learner: Teaching property through art. *The Law Teacher 11.* https://ssrn.com/abstract=587201.

1. The Birth Of Mind Maps

1. Gobonobo. (2021). *A statue resembling Lucy van Pelt outside the University of Minnesota Medical Center Emergency Room* [Photo]. Wikimedia Commons. Retrieved July 11, 2023, from https://commons.wikimedia.org/wiki/File:Statue_outside_the_University_of_Minnesota_Medical_Center_Emergency_Room.jpg
2. Peanuts Wiki. (n.d.). *Lucy's psychiatry booth.* Fandom. Retrieved July 3, 2023, from https://peanuts.fandom.com/wiki/Lucy%27s
3. Rosenberg, A. (2016, July 18). *Why you don't know your own mind.* The New York Times. https://www.nytimes.com/2016/07/18/opinion/why-you-dont-know-your-own-mind.html
4. Graziano, M. (2020, January 20). *Why you don't know your own mind.* IAI News. https://iai.tv/articles/why-you-dont-know-your-own-mind-auid-1297
5. Graziano, M. (2020, January 20). *Why you don't know your own mind.* IAI News. https://iai.tv/articles/why-you-dont-know-your-own-mind-auid-1297
6. Pikawil (2017). *Pennywise cosplay at 2017 Montreal comiccon*

[Photograph]. Wikimedia Commons. https://commons.wikimedia. org/wiki/File:Pennywise_Cosplay_3.jpg

7. Jpatokal at wts wikivoyage (2006). *Ronald McDonald goes Thai style* [Photograph]. Wikimedia Commons. https://commons.wikimedia. org/wiki/File:RonaldMcDonald_Wai.JPG

8. Frankish, K. (2016, March 27) *Whatever you think, you don't necessarily know your own mind.* Aeon. *https://aeon.co/ideas/whatever-you-think-you-don-t-necessarily-know-your-own-mind*

9. Zak, P.J. (2014, October 28).*Why your brain loves good storytelling.* Harvard Business Review. https://hbr.org/2014/10/why-your-brain-loves-good-storytelling

10. Zak, P.J. (2014, October 28).*Why your brain loves good storytelling.* Harvard Business Review. https://hbr.org/2014/10/why-your-brain-loves-good-storytelling

11. Zak, P.J. (2014, October 28).*Why your brain loves good storytelling.* Harvard Business Review. https://hbr.org/2014/10/why-your-brain-loves-good-storytelling

12. Mind Mapping (2013, August 24). *Tennis Mind Map.* Wikimedia Commons. https://commons.wikimedia.org/wiki/File:Tennis-mindmap.png. CC BY-SA 2.5

13. Potential Plus UK. (2018, June 3). *Mind Mapping.* https://potentialplusuk.org/index.php/2018/06/03

14. National Institute of Neurological Disorders and Stroke. (2023, March 24). *Brain basics: The life and death of a neuron.* https://www.ninds.nih.gov/health-information/public-education/brain-basics/brain-basics-life-and-death-neuron#

15. LadyofHats. (2007, July 12) *Complete neuron cell diagram [Vector graphics].* Wikimedia Commons. https://commons.wikimedia.org/wiki/File:Complete_neuron_cell_diagram_en.svg. Public Domain.

16. van den Berg, F. (2016, June 5). *What information do neurons actually store?* Forbes. https://www.forbes.com/sites/quora/2018/06/05/what-information-do-neurons-actually-store/?sh=2a591fd4b7ce

17. Cunnah, L. (2020, January 10) *Why mind mapping works: the benefits of mind mapping.* AYOA. https://www.ayoa.com/ourblog/why-mind-mapping-works-the-benefits-of-mind-mapping

18. Bradford, W. C. (2004). Reaching the visual learner: Teaching property through art. *The Law Teacher 11.* https://ssrn.com/abstract=587201. See also: Zopf, R. (et. al.). (2004). Attentional modulation of the human somatosensory evoked potential in a trial-by-trial spatial cueing and sustained spatial attention task measured with high density 128 channels EEG. *Cognitive Brain Research 20*(3), 491-509. https://doi.org/10.1016/j.cogbrainres.2004.02.014

19. Eisenberg, H. (2014, September 15). *Human process visual data better.* Thermopylae: Sciences + Technology. https://www.t-sciences. com/news/humans-process-visual-data-better

20. Purchotius. (1730). *Arbor Porphyrÿ (from Purchotius' Institutiones philosophicae I, 1730)* [Illustration]. Wikimedia Commons. https:// commons.wikimedia.org/wiki/File:Arbor_porphyrii_% 28from_Purchotius% 27_Institutiones_philosophicae_I,_1730%29.png. Public domain.

21. Purchotius. (1730). *Arbor Porphyrÿ (from Purchotius' Institutiones philosophicae I, 1730)* [Illustration]. Wikimedia Commons. https:// commons.wikimedia.org/wiki/File:Arbor_porphyrii_% 28from_Purchotius% 27_Institutiones_philosophicae_I,_1730%29.png. Public domain.

22. Aristotle. (1966). *Aristotle, Categories and De Interpretatione.* (Ackrill, J. Trans.) Oxford [England] at the Clarendon Press.

23. Smith, R. (1995) Logic. In J. Barnes (ed.), *The Cambridge companion to Aristotle* (p. 55). Cambridge: Cambridge University Press,

24. Finally Family Homes. (2022, July 18). *9 inspirational stories of success and overcoming obstacles.* https://finallyfamilyhomes.org/inspirational-stories-of-success/

25. RVC (2020, October 30) *Campire stories for kids.* RVC Outdoor Destinations. https://rvcoutdoors.com/campfire-stories-for-kids/

2. The Science of Mind Mapping

1. This quote is widely attributed to Coco Chanel, a French fashion designer and businesswoman. https://quotepark.com/quotes/ 1876365-coco-chanel-the-most-courageous-act-is-still-to-think-for-your/

2. Hedge, S. (2022, July 9). *What is theory of mind?* Science ABC. https://www.scienceabc.com/social-science/what-is-theory-of-mind.html

3. Byom, L.J. & Mutlu, B. (2013) Theory of mind: mechanisms, methods, and new directions. *Frontiers in Human Neuroscience, 7*(413). https://doi.org/10.3389/fnhum.2013.00413

4. Williams, J.A., Burns, E.L., & Harmon, E.A. (2009). Insincere utterances and gaze: eye contact during sarcastic statements. *Perceptual and Motor Skills, 108*(2), 565–572. https://doi.org/10. 2466/pms.108.2.565-572

5. Legerstee, M., Barna, J., & DiAdamo, C. (2000). Precursors to the development of intention at 6 months: Understanding people and

their actions. *Developmental Psychology, 36*(5), 627–634. https://doi.org/10.1037/0012-1649.36.5.627

6. Witten, I.H., Gori, M., & Numerico, T. (2006). *Web dragons: Inside the myths of search engine technology.* Morgan Kaufmann. https://doi.org/10.1016/B978-0-12-370609-6.X5000-0

7. Stok, G. (2023, April 8). *Do we need language to think?* Owlcation. The Arena Group. https://owlcation.com/humanities/thinking-thoughts-without-language

8. YG Topics. (2021, July 21). *Evolution of the human brain.* https://www.yourgenome.org/stories/evolution-of-the-human-brain/

9. Blausen.com staff (2014). Medical gallery of Blausen Medical 2014 [Illustration]. *WikiJournal of Medicine, 1*(2). https://doi.org/10.15347/wjm/2014.010

10. Mateos-Aparicio, P. & Rodriguez-Moreno, A. (2010). The Impact of Studying Brain Plasticity. *Frontiers in Cellular Neuroscience, 13*(66). https://doi.org/10.3389/fncel.2019.00066

11. Ashby, F.G. & O'Brien, J.B. (2005) Category learning and multiple memory systems. *Trends in Cognitive Sciences. 9*(2), 83–89. https://doi.org/10.1016/j.tics.2004.12.003

12. Poldrack, R.A. & Foerd,e K. (2008). Category learning and the memory systems debate. *Neuroscience and Biobehavioral Reviews, 32*(2), 197–205. https://doi.org/10.1016/j.neubiorev.2007.07.007

13. Smith, E.E. & Grossman, M. (2008). Multiple systems of category learning. *Neuroscience and Biobehavioral Reviews, 32*(2),249–264. https://doi.org/10.1016/j.neubiorev.2007.07.009

14. Huth, A.G., Nishimoto, S., Vu, A.T., & Gallant, J.L. (2012). A continuous semantic space describes the representation of thousands of object and action categories across the human brain. *Neuron,* 76(6), 1210. https://doi.org/10.1016/j.neuron.2012.10.014

15. Huffman, K. J. (2012). The developing, aging neocortex: How genetics and epigenetics influence early developmental patterning and age-related change. *Frontiers in Genetics, 3,* 212. https://doi.org/10.3389/fgene.2012.00212

16. Seger, C.A. & Miller, E.K. (2010). Category learning in the brain. *Annual Review of Neuroscience, 33,* 203-219. https://doi.org/10.1146/annurev.neuro.051508.135546

17. NeuRA Library. (2022, March 21). *Visuospatial ability.* https://library.neura.edu.au/schizophrenia/signs-and-symptoms/cognition/visuospatial-ability/#:~:text=Visuospatial%20ability

18. Knierim, J. (2020, Oct. 20) *Chapter 3: Motor cortex.* Neuroscience Online. https://nba.uth.tmc.edu/neuroscience/m/s3/

19. Anand, K.S. & Dhikav, V. (2012). Hippocampus in health and

disease: An overview. *Annals of Indian Academy of Neurology, 15*(4), 239-246. https://doi.org/10.4103/0972-2327.104323

20. Hutter, S.A. & Wilson, A.I. (2018). A novel role for the hippocampus in category learning. *The Journal of Neuroscience, 38*(31), 6803-6805. https://doi.org/10.1523/JNEUROSCI.1085-18.2018

21. O'Reilly, RC. & Munakata, Y. (McClelland, J.L.). (2000). *Computational Explorations in Cognitive Neuroscience: Understanding the Mind.* The MIT Press.

22. Wang, Y. & Ashby, F.G. (2020) A role for the medial temporal lobes in category learning. *Learning and Memory (Cold Spring Harbor, N.Y.), 27*(10), 441-450. https://doi.org/10.1101/lm.051995.120

23. Shohamy, D. & Wagner, A.D. (2008). Integrating memories in the human brain: hippocampal-midbrain encoding of overlapping events. *Neuron, 60*(2), 378–389. https://doi.org/10.1016/j.neuron.2008.09.023

24. Seger, C.A. & Spiering, B.J. (2011) A critical review of habit learning and the basal ganglia. *Frontiers in Systems Neuroscience, 5*, 66. https://doi.org/10.3389/fnsys.2011.00066

25. Seger, C.A. (2009) The involvement of corticostriatal loops in learning across tasks, species, and methodologies. In Groenewegen, H.J., et al. (Eds.). *The Basal Ganglia IX* (pp. 25-39). Advances in Behavioral Biology 58.Springer. https://doi.org/10.1007/978-1-4419-0340-2_2

26. Colder B. (2015, Sept. 23). *Cortical surface with an overlay of the basal ganglia and thalamus.* Wikimedia Commons. https://commons.wikimedia.org/wiki/File:Cortical_surface_with_an_over lay_of_the_basal_ganglia_and_thalamus.jpg. CC BY 4.0

27. Seger, C.A. (2008) How do the basal ganglia contribute to categorization? Their role in generalization, response selection, and learning via feedback. *Neuroscience and Biobehavioral Reviews, 32*(2), 265-278. https://doi.org/10.1016/j.neubiorev.2007.07.010

28. Peters, S.K., Dunlop, K., and Downar, J. (2016) Cortico-Striatal-Thalamic loop circuits of the salience network: A central pathway in psychiatric disease and treatment. *Frontiers in Systems Neuroscience, 10.* https://doi.org/10.3389/fnsys.2016.00104

29. Seger, C.A. and Spiering, B.J. (2011) A critical review of habit learning and the basal ganglia [Figure]. *Frontiers in Systems Neuroscience, 5*(66) https://doi.org/10.3389/fnsys.2011.00066. CC BY 4.0

30. Peters, S.K., Dunlop, K., and Downar, J. (2016) Cortico-Striatal-Thalamic loop circuits of the salience network: A central pathway

in psychiatric disease and treatment. *Frontiers in Systems Neuroscience*, *10*. https://doi.org/10.3389/fnsys.2016.00104

31. Cristol, H. (2021, June 14).*What is dopamine?* Web MD. https://www.webmd.com/mental-health/what-is-dopamine

32. Healthdirect Australia. (2021, April). *Dopamine.* Health Direct. https://www.healthdirect.gov.au/dopamine#

33. Lee, D., Seo, H., & Jung, M. W. (2012). Neural Basis of Reinforcement Learning and Decision Making. *Annual Review of Neuroscience*, *35*(1), 287-308. https://doi.org/10.1146/annurev-neuro-062111-150512

34. Glimcher, P.W. (2011). Understanding dopamine and reinforcement learning: The dopamine reward prediction error hypothesis. *Proceedings of the National Academy of Sciences*, *108*(3), 15647-15654, https://doi.org/10.1073/pnas.101426910

35. Cai, J., & Tong, Q. (2022). Anatomy and function of ventral tegmental area glutamate neurons. *Frontiers in Neural Circuits*, *16*(867053). https://doi.org/10.3389/fncir.2022.867053

36. Becker, B. (n.d.) *How memories are made: Stages of memory formation.* Lesley University. https://lesley.edu/article/stages-of-memory#

37. Krames, C. (2009). *Drawing illustrating the process of synaptic transmission in neurons, cropped from original in an NIA brochure* [Illustration]. Wikimedia Commons. https://commons.wikimedia.org/wiki/File:Chemical_synapse_schema_cropped.jpg

38. Pappas, S. (2022, September 27). *How does the brain store memories?* Live Science. https://www.livescience.com/how-the-brain-stores-memories

39. User:Washington irving. (2004, February). *Hippocampus* [Vector graphics]. Wikimedia commons. https://commons.wikimedia.org/wiki/File:Hippocampus.png

40. Seress, L. (1980). *Hippocampus and seahorse* [Photograph]. Wikimedia commons. https://commons.wikimedia.org/wiki/File:Hippocampus_and_seahorse.JPG. CC BY-SA 1.0

41. McGaugh, J. L., Cahill, L., & Roozendaal, B. (1996). Involvement of the amygdala in memory storage: Interaction with other brain systems. *Proceedings of the National Academy of Sciences*, *93*(24), 13508-13514. https://doi.org/10.1073/pnas.93.24.13508

42. Hermans, E.J., Battaglia, F.P., Atsak, P., de Voogd, L.D., Fernández, G., & Roozendaal, B. (2014). How the amygdala affects emotional memory by altering brain network properties. *Neurobiology of Learning and Memory*, *112*, 2-16. https://doi.org/10.1016/j.nlm.2014.02.005

3. Mastering Memory

1. Foley, E. (2022, February 16). *105 sample Jeopardy! questions to test your skills*. Trivia Bliss. https://triviabliss.com/examples-of-jeopardy-questions/
2. Hopper, C. (2000) *Practicing college study skills: Strategies for success* (2nd ed.). Houghton Mifflin College Div.
3. Chen, C. (2019, October 21). *Studying in new spaces*. Mullen Memory. https://mullenmemory.com/memory-palace/studying-in-new-spaces
4. Chen, C. (2019, October 21). *Studying in new spaces*. Mullen Memory. https://mullenmemory.com/memory-palace/studying-in-new-spaces
5. University of Pittsburgh. (2023, April 14). *Active memorization*. https://www.asundergrad.pitt.edu/study-lab/active-memorization#
6. Yates, F. A. (1966). *The art of memory*. University of Chicago Press
7. Wei, X. (2021, November). *Proactive interference caused by repeated use of memory palace*. Southern Illinois University Carbondale, OpenSIUC.
8. University of Pittsburgh. (2023, April 14). *Active memorization*. https://www.asundergrad.pitt.edu/study-lab/active-memorization#
9. Higbee, K. L. (2001). *Your Memory: How it Works and How to Improve It* (2nd ed.). Da Capo Lifelong Books.
10. Quershi, A., Rizvi, F., Syed, A., Shahid, A., & Manzoor, H. (2014) The method of loci as a mnemonic device to facilitate learning in endocrinology leads to improvement in student performance as measured by assessments. *AJP Advances in Physiology Education, 38*(2), 140-144. https://doi.org/10.1152/advan.00092.2013
11. Mind Tools Ltd. (n.d.). *The journey technique*. https://www.mindtools.com/a2ahpip/the-journey-technique

4. Overcoming Mind Map Challenges

1. Cunningham, J. (2021, January 22). *The Tao of success*. Medium. https://medium.com/be-somebody/the-tao-of-success-7a1aa7199b14
2. MindMapping.com. (n.d.). *What is a mind map?* https://www.mindmapping.com/mind-map#
3. BruceBlaus. (2013, September 30). *Multipolar neuron* [Vector Graphics]. https://commons.wikimedia.org/wiki/File:Blausen CC BY 3.0

4. Fernandosca. (2018, April 12). *Memorize mind map* [Illustration]. https://commons.wikimedia.org/wiki/File: Memorize_mind_map.png. CC BY-SA 4.0

5. Mayfield Certified Health Info. (2018). *Anatomy of the brain.* Mayfield Brain & Spine. https://d3djccaurgtij4.cloudfront.net/pe-anatomybrain.pdf

6. Wilson, K., Copeland-Solas, E., & Guthrie-Dixon, N. (2016). A preliminary study on the use of mind mapping as a visual learning strategy in general education science classes for Arabic speakers in the United Arab Emirates. *Journal of the Scholarship of Teaching and Learning, 16*(1), 31-52, https://doi.org/10.14434/josotl.v16i1.19181

7. Wilson, K., Copeland-Solas, E., & Guthrie-Dixon, N. (2016). A preliminary study on the use of mind mapping as a visual learning strategy in general education science classes for Arabic speakers in the United Arab Emirates. *Journal of the Scholarship of Teaching and Learning, 16*(1), 31-52, https://doi.org/10.14434/josotl.v16i1.19181

8. Elsayed, A.A., Eldiasty, N.E.M.M., El Salam, F.A.M.A., Mohamed, S.H., & Younes, M.M.A.E. (2022) Effect of using mind mapping learning technique among undergraduate nursing students. *Egyptian Journal of Health Care, 13*(4),1375-1384. https://doi.org/10.21608/ejhc.2022.270425

9. MindMapping.com. (n.d.). *What is a mind map?* https://www.-mindmapping.com/mind-map#

10. Lynch, A. (n.d.). *Mind map for note taking – 4 practical practices.* EDraw: A Wondershare Company. https://www.edrawsoft.com/mindmaster/mind-map-note-taking-practice.html

11. Kalyanasundaram, M., Abraham, S.B., Ramachandran, D., Jayaseelan, V., Bazroy, J., Singh, Z., & Purty, A.J. (2017). Effectiveness of mind mapping technique in information retrieval among medical college students in Puducherry-A pilot study. *Indian Journal of Community Medicine, 42(1),*19-23. https://doi.org/10.4103/0970-0218.199793

12. Janice. (n.d.). *What is a mind map?* EDraw: A Wondershare Company. https://www.edrawsoft.com/mind-map-definition.html

13. Vicwood40. (2005, January 27). *Conceptmap* [Vector Graphics]. Wikimedia commons. https://en.wikipedia.org/wiki/File: Conceptmap.gif#/media/File:Conceptmap.png. CC BY-SA 3.0

14. University of Buffalo. (n.d.) *Constructivism.* Office of Curriculum Assessment and Teaching Transformation. https://www.buffalo.edu/catt/develop/theory/constructivism.html

15. Frey, C. (n.d.). 5 powerful ways to manage large, complex mind maps. *The Mind Mapping Software Blog.* https://

mindmappingsoftwareblog.com/manage-large-complex-mind-maps/

16. Alsuraihi, A. (2022). The effect of implementing mind maps for online learnings and assessment on students during COVID-19 pandemic: a cross sectional study. *BMC Medical Education, 22*(1), 169. https://doi.org/10.1186/s12909-022-03211-2

5. Mind Map Mastery

1. Brown, M. (2015, November 19). *Classmates turns 20: How the social network missed an opportunity to be Facebook*. GeekWire. https://www.geekwire.com/2015/classmates/

2. Empire State University. (n.d.) *Clustering/Mapping*. https://www.sunyempire.edu/online-writing-support/resources/academic-writing/process/prewriting-developing-ideas/clustering/mapping/#

3. Alexander, T. (2018, October 30). Spencer, E. (Ed.). *How to work best with the 4 different types of learners*. Work Life, Atlassian. https://www.atlassian.com/blog/teamwork/how-to-work-4-different-learning-types#

4. Heinrich, A.V. (n.d.). *Japan: Timeline of Historical Periods*. ASIA for Educators, Columbia University. http://afe.easia.columbia.edu/timelines/japan_timeline.htm

6. Putting Mind Maps In Action

1. This is widely attributed to Jeff Duntemann, author. Quote Master, (n.d.) https://www.quotemaster.org/q5be9c0adcaaa16c6205866b3369c1d96

2. Jetkasettakorn, S. (n.d.). *Thai style wood carving Free Photo* [Photograph]. Vecteezy. https://www.vecteezy.com/photo/9587371-thai-style-wood-carving

7. Choose Your Own Map

1. Lam, W. (2015, November 10). *Baskin Robbins Classic One Scoop Sundae (22767474120)* [Photograph]. Wikimedia Commons. https://commons.wikimedia.org/wiki/File:Baskin_Robbins_Classic_One_Scoop_Sundae_%2822767474120%29.jpg. CC BY-SA 2.0

2. Ben & Jerry's Homemade, Inc. (2018, July 3). *10 Presidents who loved ice cream.* https://www.benjerry.com/whats-new/2017/01/presidents-and-ice-cream

3. Baskin-Robbins. (n.d.) *Fun facts.* https://baskinrobbins.com.sg/content/baskinrobbins

4. "Fact Sheets." (2023) *Baskin-Robbins Newsroom.* https://news.baskinrobbins.com/about

5. Ghosal, G. (2021, December 22). *8 types of mind maps you need to know about.* Make Use Of. https://www.makeuseof.com/types-of-mind-maps-to-know/

6. Anderson, C. (n.d.). *Flow Mapping.* PennState College of Earth and Mineral Sciences, The Pennsylvania State University. https://www.e-education.psu.edu/geog486/node/679

7. Alexander, T. (2018, October 30). Spencer, E. (Ed.). *How to work best with the 4 different types of learners.* Work Life, Atlassian. https://www.atlassian.com/blog/teamwork/how-to-work-4-different-learning-types#

8. Alexander, T. (2018, October 30). Spencer, E. (Ed.). *How to work best with the 4 different types of learners.* Work Life, Atlassian. https://www.atlassian.com/blog/teamwork/how-to-work-4-different-learning-types#

9. Alexander, T. (2018, October 30). Spencer, E. (Ed.). *How to work best with the 4 different types of learners.* Work Life, Atlassian. https://www.atlassian.com/blog/teamwork/how-to-work-4-different-learning-types#

10. Dykeman, M. (n.d.). *Four ways mind maps make you more creative.* Lateral Action. https://lateralaction.com/articles/mind-maps/?cn-reloaded=1

8. Preparation, Execution, and Interpretation

1. Katelaris, E. (2023, May 9). *My son's school had an 'emergency meeting' for his disturbing drawing — but it was all a misunderstanding* [News post and Photograph]. New York Post. https://nypost.com/2023/05/09/my-sons-school-had-an-emergency-meeting-for-his-disturbing-drawing-but-it-was-all-a-misunderstanding/

2. Gallero-Salas, Y., Han, S., Sych, Y., Voigt, F.F., Laurenczy, B., Gilad, A., & Helmchen, F. (2020). Sensory and behavioral components of neocortical signal flow in discrimination tasks with short-term memory. *Neuron, 109*(1), 135-148, https://doi.org/10.1016/j.neuron.2020.10.017

3. Seger, C.A. & Miller, E.K. (2010). Category learning in the brain. *Annual Review of Neuroscience, 33*(1), 203–219. https://doi.org/10.1146/annurev.neuro.051508.135546
4. EdrawMind: A Wondershare Company (https://www.edrawsoft.com/)

9. Mind Mapping For The Modern Times

1. Anderson, J. & Rainie, L. (2018, July 3). *Stories from experts about the impact of digital life.* Pew Research Center. https://www.pewresearch.org/internet/2018/07/03/stories-from-experts-about-the-impact-of-digital-life/
2. Frey, C. (n.d.) 5 powerful ways to manage large, complex mind maps. *The Mind Mapping Software Blog.* https://mindmappingsoftwareblog.com/manage-large-complex-mind-maps/
3. All ratings were obtained from GetApp Mind Mapping Software (2023) *Mind mapping software.* Retrieved June 8, 2023, from https://www.getapp.com/collaboration-software/mind-mapping/
4. Miro Home (https://miro.com/mind-map/)
5. Lucidspark (https://lucidspark.com)
6. G2.com, Inc. (n.d.). *Lucidspark reviews and product details.* Retrieved June 8, 2023, from https://www.g2.com/products/lucidspark/reviews
7. PeerSpot. (n.d.). *Lucidspark reviews.* Retrieved June 8, 2023, from https://www.peerspot.com/products/lucidspark-reviews
8. Brandner, R. (n.d.). Looking back on 10 years of web design. *MindMeister.* https://www.mindmeister.com/blog/10-years-web-design-history/#
9. MeisterLabs. (n.d.) "All the Features." Mind Meister. Retrieved June 8, 2023, from https://www.mindmeister.com/pages/features/
10. Software Testing Help. (2023, July 7). *10 best mind mapping software in 2023 (Top selective).* https://www.softwaretestinghelp.com/mind-map-software/#:~:text=Cacoo%20is%20a%20user%2Dfriendly
11. Cacoo by Nulab. (n.d.). *Mind mapping software: Create mind maps online with Cacoo.* https://nulab.com/cacoo/examples/mind-mapping-software/?utm_source=capterra&utm_medium=affiliate&utm_campaign=mind_mapping&capterra_ppc=GetApp
12. LiquidText. (n.d.). *Better than paper.* Retrieved June 8, 2023, from. https://www.liquidtext.net/
13. Hiemstra, P. (2021, June 27). LiquidText is a great way to do your

research. *Medium.* https://medium.com/@p.h.hiemstra/liquidtext-is-a-great-way-to-do-your-research-d04f17dae36d

14. Dang, A. (n.d.). Learning technologies: Trello, LiquidText, and Notability. *Ohio State University.* Retrieved June 8, 2023, from https://u.osu.edu/dang159hseportfolio/learning-technologies/#

15. Edwards, L. (2022, May 9). *What is Padlet and how does it work? Tips and tricks.* Tech&Learning. https://www.techlearning.com/how-to/what-is-padlet-and-how-does-it-work-for-teachers-and-students

16. Sondgeroth, B. (2017, October 6). *Padlet: collaborative and multimedia mind mapping tool.* EdTechTeacher. https://edtechteacher.org/padlet-collaborative-multimedia-mind-mapping-tool/#

17. EdrawMind (https://www.edrawsoft.com/ad/edrawmind/)

18. EdrawMind. (2021, September 10). In Wikitia. https://wikitia.com/wiki/EdrawMind#

19. Wondershare. (2023, May 31). *Wondershare EdrawMind launched its one click solution with an upgraded artificial intelligence feature* [Press release]. https://www.prnewswire.com/news-releases/wondershare-edrawmind-launched-its-one-click-solution-with-an-upgraded-artificial-intelligence-feature-301838353.html

Afterword

1. This is a quote attributed to Andrew Ng, a British-American computer scientist retrieved June 8, 2023, from *BrainyQuote* (https://www.brquote.com/topics/complexity-quotes)

2. Seals and Croft. (1977). My Fair Share [Song]. On *ONE ON ONE.* Warner Bros. Records. Music by Charles Fox, lyrics by Paul Williams.

DISCLAIMER

The information contained in this book and its components, is meant to serve as a comprehensive collection of strategies that the author of this book has done research about. Summaries, strategies, tips and tricks are only recommendations by the author, and reading this book will not guarantee that one's results will exactly mirror the author's results.

The author of this book has made all reasonable efforts to provide current and accurate information for the readers of this book. The author and their associates will not be held liable for any unintentional errors or omissions that may be found, and for damages arising from the use or misuse of the information presented in this book.

Readers should exercise their own judgment and discretion in interpreting and applying the information to their specific circumstances. This book is not intended to replace professional advice (especially medical advice, diagnosis, or treatment). Readers are encouraged to seek appropriate professional guidance for their individual needs.

The material in the book may include information by third parties. Third party materials comprise of opinions expressed by their owners. As such, the author of this book does not assume responsibility or liability for any third party material or opinions.

The publication of third party material does not constitute the author's guarantee of any information, products, services, or opinions contained within third party material. Use of third party material does not guarantee that your results will mirror our results. Publication of such third party material is simply a recommendation and expression of the author's own opinion of that material.

Whether because of the progression of the Internet, or the unforeseen changes in company policy and editorial submission guidelines, what is stated as fact at the time of this writing may become outdated or inapplicable later.

Wisdom University is committed to respecting copyright laws and intellectual property rights. We have taken reasonable measures to ensure that all quotes, diagrams, figures, images, tables, and other information used in this publication are either created by us, obtained with permission, or fall under fair use guidelines. However, if any copyright infringement has inadvertently occurred, please notify us promptly at wisdom-university@mail.net, providing sufficient details to identify the specific material in question. We will take immediate action to rectify the situation, which may include obtaining necessary permissions, making corrections, or removing the material in subsequent editions or reprints.

Made in United States
Orlando, FL
13 July 2024

48821659R00136